WEALTH *to*
LAST

THE BURKETT & BLUE

DEFINITIVE *Guide* TO SECURING

WEALTH *to* LAST

MONEY ESSENTIALS *for the* SECOND HALF OF LIFE

LARRY BURKETT
RON BLUE

With JEREMY WHITE, CPA

BROADMAN
&HOLMAN
PUBLISHERS

NASHVILLE, TENNESSEE

0-8054-2785-6

Published by Broadman & Holman Publishers,
Nashville, Tennessee

Dewey Decimal Classification: 332.024
Subject Heading: PERSONAL FINANCE \ SAVING AND
THRIFT \ STEWARDSHIP

The authors are represented by the literary agency of
Wolgemuth & Associates, Inc.

Unless otherwise stated all Scripture citation is from the NASB,
The New American Standard Bible, © The Lockman Foundation,
1960, 1962, 1963, 1968, 1971, 1972, 1973, 1975, 1977, 1995, used
by permission. Other passages are noted as NIV, the Holy Bible, New
International Version, © 1973, 1978, 1984 by International Bible
Society; and KJV, King James Version.

1 2 3 4 5 6 7 8 9 10 07 06 05 04 03

ACKNOWLEDGMENTS

Larry Burkett went home to be with the Lord on July 4, 2003, one week after we finished all work on this book. He was a friend, mentor, and fellow disciple of Jesus Christ. I will miss him more than I even know for all of the influence he had on my life. This book would never have happened apart from Larry's vision to see it happen. He had more impact on the kingdom of Christ than anyone else in our generation, and it was a privilege to know him and coauthor a book with him. I, of course, also want to acknowledge Jeremy White for his ability to pull together the different thinking and writing styles that Larry and I possess into a book that communicates clearly the message that we desire to communicate. Lastly, I want to acknowledge my assistant, Sherry Lantis, who has kept me on track with so many things over so many years, including this book.

—Ron Blue

My contribution to this book could never have happened without the help of others. Foremost, I want to thank the Lord for enabling me to glean insights from the inexhaustible riches of His Word. And I want to thank Ron Blue and Jeremy White for lending their wisdom and technical expertise to this project. I am also grateful for the invaluable help provided by Deb Smith, my personal assistant, and Adeline Griffith, my editor.

—Larry Burkett

Two of the pioneers in applying common sense, Biblical principles, and practical wisdom to personal finances are Larry Burkett and Ron Blue. They both inspired me in the 1980's to integrate the wisdom from the Bible to my professional background. In addition, to their teaching, my parents and grandparents lived out the practical, financial wisdom of living within their means, minimizing debt, and giving. I would also like to thank a great support team: Pam Estes, Sharon White, Chip Thomas, and Kris White.

—Jeremy White, CPA

CONTENTS

INTRODUCTION
— OR —
"Why Write Another Financial Book?"

You should have two financial goals in life: to make a little money first,
and then to make a little money last.

UNKNOWN

Courage is not the absence of fear, but rather the judgment that something else is more important than fear.

AMBROSE REDMOON

Instruct those who are rich in this present world not to be conceited or
to fix their hope on the uncertainty of riches, but on God, who richly
supplies us with all things to enjoy. Instruct them to do good, to be
rich in good works, to be generous and ready to share, storing up for
themselves the treasure of a good foundation for the future, so that
they may take hold of that which is life indeed.

1 TIMOTHY 6:17–19

Over the last thirty years, we have written many financial books between the two of us. They focus on the biblical principles of managing money. Because these biblical principles are God's timeless principles, they apply to all ages and stages of life.

So why write another financial book? Haven't we said it all before? We grappled with these questions because it is no easy chore to write. Believe us, we have other activities we prefer more than writing—just as you likely have other interests besides reading financial books!

Here is what we have observed during the last few years. In the United States of America, the most prosperous country in the world by any measure, we see financial fear. We see more fear in the age group of fifty and over. On a positive note we see more potential for God's Kingdom in this same age group. Our goal with this book is to help people with their fear, their worry, and their stewardship potential.

We regularly hear real-life examples from callers to Larry's *Money Matters* radio programs as well as from attendees at Ron's investment seminars. They show deep financial concern.

- A fifty-four-year-old manager at a Fortune 500 company has a recurring ulcer when opening his 401(k) statements each quarter. His 401(k), made up of company stock and growth mutual funds, has plummeted from $300,000 to $140,000. He figures he will have to work five years longer than planned.

- A retired couple is not as free as they had expected. They realize they are sandwiched between generations needing help. Their aging parents require in-home care and will use up all their resources if admitted to a nursing home. Their adult children need financial help after recent divorces.

- A married fifty-nine-year-old woman is anxious about debt. Previously debt-free, she and her husband borrowed $100,000 against their house to invest in the rising stock market in early

2000. He was going to "make a killing in the market" and retire sooner. Their stock portfolio is down to $40,000 while their mortgage is more than twice that much.

* A seventy-two-year-old widow has seen her income drop as interest rates drop on her bank certificates of deposits. She depends on the interest income to make ends meet. Now she is dipping into her principal and is afraid she will outlive her money.

These examples are why we write, why we speak, why we teach, and why we record radio broadcasts. We want to help.

Recent surveys show that help is needed. Seventy-four percent of baby boomers believe they are financially prepared for retirement. But 59 percent expect to carry debt of some form into retirement, and 46 percent have saved less than $50,000 towards retirement.[1] The perception looks better than reality.

The American Society of Pension Actuaries found that more than 50 percent of pre-retirees underestimate their life expectancy. According to mortality tables, a married couple at age sixty-five have a 67-percent chance that both will live to age eighty-five. There's a 33-percent chance that one will make it to age ninety. Will your wealth last that long?

This book is different from our other books because it is targeted toward the specific age group of fifty and older. Those fifty and over are either the nearly retired, newly retired, rarely retired, or nearly retired out of retirement. We are in the same demographic group as the target audience of our book, so we personally understand your financial concerns and issues. We deal with the same issues of how to invest in an uncertain economy and stock market, when or how to retire, when to start Social Security, and how best to help adult children.

Some of the wisest counsel I (Larry) ever received was from a professor I had in graduate school. He taught economics and regularly said, "Answer the questions that people are asking. The majority of people answer questions that nobody asks."

So, when we considered what people fifty and older are asking us, we broadly grouped their questions into the following categories.

THE "NOW WHAT?" QUESTIONS

These questions come in two forms. The first type of "now what?" question is along the lines of: "Given what has happened in the stock market or the economy, now what? Now what do I do with my investments, my retirement plans, my pension choices, or health insurance?" In this book we will address the current state of the economy and the stock market. Regardless of the current economic scenario, we want to help you grip principles instead of being gripped by fear.

The other type of "now what?" question is more of a "what's next?" inquiry. Much of our teaching over the last four decades has focused on the financial fundamentals of budgeting, avoiding credit card debt, and saving. We are honored and humbled to learn that many have successfully applied our advice—which we admit we plagiarized from God's Word—and benefited from it.

Many have moved beyond budgeting. They have paid off credit cards, bought houses, and raised families. They want to go to the next level of stewardship. They are asking, "Now what?" We have devoted separate chapters to discuss the more advanced topics of investments, retirement issues, long-term care insurance, and estate planning.

THE "FOR MY SITUATION, HOW DO I DECIDE ABOUT _____?" QUESTIONS

Most people are interested in help for their own specific situation. While we often enjoy considering government policy issues or macroeconomic issues, most people are not asking these general questions. Therefore, the focus of this book is personal application.

However, your financial decisions are affected by the economy. So we will examine the current economy and stock market in chapter 1. These form the backdrop or setting for many of the targeted financial issues and principles we will discuss throughout the book.

The financial decisions faced by those of us fifty and older are more critical than earlier ones of whether to buy a new or used vehicle or to reduce the entertainment budget. They are critical because some are irrevocable. For example, you only decide once how to receive your pension distribution. Also, significant dollars are involved. A 401(k) or IRA may be the largest asset you own, so you must consider carefully its investment, rollover, or ultimately its distribution. Time is an asset for those under fifty, but for those over fifty, time is not on our side. There is less time to make up stock losses, less time to earn an income, less time to recover from mistakes.

THE "WHAT ARE YOU PERSONALLY DOING?" QUESTIONS

As financial counselors and teachers, we regularly advise others what to do. In doing so, we often ask people questions. Sometimes people turn the tables and quiz us. "Larry and Ron, tell me how you are personally handling _____?" For example, people regularly ask if we do in fact budget in our household. (See chapter 7 for the answer.) Such questions may be a test of our integrity or simply a desire to hear an example or an application of a financial principle.

At the end of each chapter, we have provided two question-and-answer sections. The first section is called "Ask Larry and Ron." Here we include personal and direct questions toward how we handle certain financial matters within our own households. We face the same issues this book addresses. Although each person faces unique circumstances, we hope our personal experiences will help you.

The "Ask Larry and Ron" questions will also include general questions received from others similar to you. Using this case-study approach, we hope to apply and reiterate the key concepts in each chapter.

We call the second section of questions "Ask Yourself." We will ask you questions to consider. Rather than just reading for information purposes, we try to hold you accountable to apply the information. That's wisdom—information applied to life. Reflect on these questions, pray about them, and discuss them with your family.

When we identified the common theme of all the types of questions, when we boiled down the various fears into one, we concluded it is this: "Will I outlive my money?" Variations of this theme or fear are "Will I have enough?" or "Will my wealth last?"

This has long been the overriding fear as people grow older.

Several thousand years ago a widowed woman had the same fear. Her creditors, demanding payment of her bills, were about to take her sons as slaves to pay off the debt. Her assets were exhausted except for a jar of oil.

Her husband had been employed by Elisha, a prophet of God. So the widow met with Elisha to ask for help. Elisha didn't offer fringe benefits of a 401(k), a profit-sharing plan, or group term-life insurance for employees and their dependents. But he did offer a plan of provision.

Elisha worked with what she had and instructed her, "Go around and ask your neighbors for empty jars. Not just a few, but a lot. Then, behind closed doors, start pouring your oil into the jars."

The widow and her sons did as Elisha instructed them. The oil kept flowing. From her initial amount to the top of the rim on the first jar it kept flowing. It filled all the jars they had gathered. A pretty good return on her initial investment of oil.

She returned to Elisha to tell him what had happened. He told her to sell the oil and pay her debts. Then he said that she and her sons could live on what was left.[2]

Her wealth lasted. What did it take for that to happen? Some of her own actions, some faith, and God's provision. What did the widow do?

- *She knew her current situation.* She was aware of her debts and aware of her limited assets.
- *She sought answers and help.* Rather than simply worry, she took action.
- *She went to the right source for help.* Instead of listening to all the other worrying widows at the well or getting financial advice from her hairstylist, she went to Elisha for godly counsel.
- *She obeyed.* The prophet's unusual advice didn't sound so profitable. This was not how her mother or grandmother had done it. But she obeyed and benefited.
- *She participated in the economy.* Although her story is mainly one of God's miraculous provision, she still had to acquire jars, price the oil, advertise the oil, sell the oil, collect the money, pay off the debtors, and allocate the rest of the proceeds.

God is our ultimate Sustainer and Provider. But, like the widow, you will need to take action.

You likely have more assets available than a jar of oil. But the fear of those assets lasting is still relevant. Consider the recent trends of increased longevity, lower interest rates, higher health insurance costs, declining stock market returns, and higher nursing home costs.

Will your wealth last? What must you do for your wealth to last? Our answers are inside this book. They ultimately are inside God's Book, the Bible.

Let's start with the final observation in the widow's story. She responded to and followed through on God's provision by operating within her economy and marketplace. So must you.

CHAPTER 1

IS THIS ECONOMY DIFFERENT?
— OR —
"Getting a Grip on the Slippery, Sliding Economy"

Right now I'm having amnesia and déjà vu at the same time. I think I've forgotten this before.

STEVEN WRIGHT

Human beings, who are almost unique in having the ability to learn from the experience of others, are also remarkable for their apparent disinclination to do so.

DOUGLAS ADAMS

For whatever was written in earlier times was written for our instruction, that through perseverance and the encouragement of the Scriptures we might have hope.

ROMANS 15:4

Search me, O God, and know my heart; try me and know my anxious thoughts. And see if there be any hurtful way in me, and lead me in the everlasting way.

PSALM 139:23–24

J ohn clenches his teeth and his newspaper as he reads the headlines of another gut-wrenching decline in the stock market. "I can't believe it," he angrily blurts out to no one in particular.

"What did you say, dear?" his wife, Mary, asks as she enters the den from the kitchen, still drying the last dinner plate.

"Oh, nothing, really," John tries to sound in control. He tells a white lie, "I am just a little concerned about the stock market and the economy." He scans the other articles of corporate corruption, unemployment on the rise, and a likely recession.

"Well, we are OK, aren't we?" Mary anxiously inquires.

After meeting with his stockbroker last week, John knew their portfolio of popular growth company stocks was down 40 percent from the initial amount invested. He had not told Mary yet. Forty percent! His stomach was in knots when he thought about how long it took to earn and save that 40 percent he had lost.

"We are down some," he finally replies unconvincingly. She usually seems to know when he is spinning the news.

Her lower lip trembling, Mary tries her best to hold back an "I told you so" along with her tears. "How much money have we lost? You had told me that these investments would help us meet all our financial dreams."

"I don't understand how it is happening. The fellows at work had been bragging in recent years about how much they were making. Some had even quit and retired early. Well, Mary, you even heard for yourself at the Smiths' Christmas party last year. Remember the talk about stock gains funding their vacations and new houses?"

"You promised that we were not going to do anything risky." Her voice changed to tears. "What about your retiring? What about Johnny's last year in college?"

"I didn't think these companies were risky. Railroads have done well for several years. These are the 1870s. I thought we had learned our lessons from the great 'Panic of 1857.'"

Conversations like this one have likely happened every decade or so in American homes. If we change from railroad companies to Internet or telecommunication companies, we have the script for the heated family discussions in the early 2000s. As Yogi Berra said, "It's déjà vu all over again."

After the Civil War the railroads connected the coasts and provided the infrastructure for a growing economy. Railroad stocks were hot. People made outstanding returns for a while. Railroads seemed like a "sure thing" as their potential would build the bridge into the next century. The bubble burst, helped by some corporate corruption at several major railroads, and many people lost most of their investments. This led to a prolonged stock market downturn and general economic weakness throughout the 1870s.[1]

The recent weakness of the stock market and the economy may seem new and different to you. This is natural because, depending on your age, you may never have experienced this type of economy. The truth is, however, it looks like, smells like, and walks like sluggish markets and economies of the past.

Solomon, no doubt an astute economist, said,

What has been will be again,

what has been done will be done again;

there is nothing new under the sun.

Is there anything of which one can say,

"Look! This is something new"?

It was here already, long ago;

it was here before our time. (Ecclesiastes 1:9–10 NIV)

An expression that our children and grandchildren use is "Get a grip!" The context for using this expression is when someone is overreacting. He or she is out of touch with reality or needs to calm down. (We must say that the younger generation often directs the "Get a grip!" expression toward us, but it could often be redirected to them!) Using the typical phrasing of financial advisers and consultants, we would define "getting a grip" as "maintaining the proper long-term perspective."

A grip is designed to help you handle an object or stabilize yourself when in a difficult spot. Here are five truths, or "grips," to help you handle the current challenging economy.

GRIP 1: ECONOMIES AND STOCK MARKETS GO UP AND DOWN.

The preceeding may seem like an overstatement of the obvious. But in the late 1990s many Wall Street analysts and some politicians were fond of saying that we have entered a new era of uninterrupted growth. They believed that the Internet companies and other new technologies were leading us to a new plateau, leaving behind the old cycles of growth and recession.

Some have said that economic history is the wrong opinions of dead men. But we tend to agree with George Santayana who said, "Those who cannot remember the past are doomed to repeat it." Historical norms are not artificial restrictions. They are the normal way markets and economies tend to function. When the economy defies logic (in a positive or a negative sense), it tends to right itself. If it's up for extended periods, then it will likely go down. If it's down, then it will come back up.

A completed *business cycle* is the period from the peak growth through the lowest point, or trough, to the next peak. It is the term for the ups and downs. If you were born in 1945, then you have lived through nine business cycles. From 1854 to the present, economists have identified thirty-one business cycles.[2]

So grasp that grip. The U.S. economy has been down thirty-one times since 1854. That's once about every five years on average. After each of those thirty-one downturns, it has returned to an upward growth cycle every time.

The current recession that began in March 2001 came on the heels of the longest economic expansion on record, from March 1991 to March 2001.[3] The long period of good economic times spoiled us. It made the correction period feel worse, but there is nothing new under the sun.

The stock market also had an incredible run from 1991 to March 2000. Let's say that Jill invested $10,000 on September 30, 1991, in large, well-established companies and $10,000 in aggressive companies focused on technology. Here's how she would have fared:

	Initial Investment at 9/30/91		Ending Value at 3/31/2000
Large companies—growth	$10,000	⇒	$46,566[4]
Smaller, high-tech companies—aggressive growth	$10,000	⇒	$86,791[5]

Wow, markets certainly can go up! The combined total return for both investments was a whopping 567 percent for the entire period.

Let's say that Jack saw how well Jill was doing. He wanted to get those same outstanding returns. But Jack didn't understand that markets go both up and down. He thought the up period would continue indefinitely. If Jack invested $10,000 on April 1, 2000, in the same investments as Jill, here's how he would have fared:

	Initial Investment at 4/01/2000		Ending Value at 9/30/2002
Large companies—growth	$10,000	⇒	$5,633[6]
Smaller, high-tech companies—aggressive growth	$10,000	⇒	$2,563[7]

Needless to say, Jack doesn't enjoy opening his quarterly statements. Jack learned the hard way that markets can and will go down.

From every past recession, from every past down market, there has been a recovery. With our human emotions we err in our optimism by assuming that the good times will always continue. Or in our pessimism we assume the bad times will continue. In truth, you should be prepared for the normal, perfectly normal, up and down periods.

GRIP 2: THE ONLY CERTAINTY IS UNCERTAINTY.

We may know and accept that economies and markets go up and down. What we really wish to know is *when* and *how much* they will go up and down. Those are the unanswerable questions that so many seek to answer.

Knowing that the only certainty is uncertainty, we both have tried to avoid being forecasters. But people, in their desire to know when the market will turn around, continually have pressed us for predictions. No matter the caveats or disclaimers we give, people focus only on our specific "when" or "how much" prediction.

For example, I (Larry) wrote a book in 1991 called *The Coming Economic Earthquake.* Looking at the trends of increasing government spending and rising consumer debt, I wrote that, in my opinion, disastrous economic consequences would result unless we made changes.

But everyone wanted to know when the earthquake would hit. I never gave an exact date; I simply said it was coming. Some misinterpreted my analysis and comments to mean an economic earthquake would hit in 1993 or 1995 or 1997. I did mention that a possible seventy-year cycle from the Great Depression would place a possible next depression around 2000. I also used a fictitious scenario based in 1999 of what economic chaos would look like in our daily lives.

Was I right about the economic earthquake? Well, yes and no. Many of the trends I saw in 1991 changed for the better with a newly elected Congress in 1994. This new Congress reduced spending and aimed to reduce the deficits. With spending constraints and an improving economy, the annual deficits lowered. Inflation did not happen as I anticipated. I had no way of knowing the dramatic improvements in productivity brought about by the Internet and other technological advances. We have experienced a significant decline in our stock market. Many other economies in the world, such as Japan and Russia, have experienced economic earthquakes.

The key point is that even with the best of minds and best of intentions no one knows the future. When I wrote *Crisis Control* in 1999, I predicted the stock market could not continue going up as it had in recent years. I was right on the money. I also said that computer problems resulting from Y2K would cause isolated and frustrating outages and shortages. Small businesses might fail because of business disruption. None of that happened. OK, my predictions are about the same as flipping a coin. I never claimed to be a prophet.

Even when we are trying to be cautious about predictions, we can end up being wrong. In 1992, I (Ron) wrote a book called *Storm Shelter: Protecting Your Personal Finances*. Being aware of this grip, I made great efforts not to make any predictions. For the most part, I succeeded except for one brief, almost offhand comment: "Today's inflation rate is around 3 percent. After experiencing 13 percent inflation in 1980, the 3 percent level seems quite acceptable. But it is not likely to last."

Now I would imagine that 99 percent of the U.S. population would have agreed with that statement at the time. Americans had experienced average annual inflation in the 1980s of 5.6 percent. In the 1970s, inflation was even higher: a 7.1 percent average annual rate. But in the ten years that followed my forecast in 1992, inflation was near 3 percent every single year! In fact, it was more than 3 percent in only one year.[8] Even what appears to be an obvious or safe prediction may not necessarily be so. As an old proverb says, "Forecasting is very difficult—especially about the future."

We do not know what will cause the next upturn or the next downturn or when it will happen. "The economy is constantly feeding us surprises," stated former Federal Reserve Vice Chairman Alan Blinder. The oil crisis of 1973–74 shocked our economy and stock markets. The Internet and technology boom fueled the 1990s. Y2K caused hardly a ripple, but a few terrorists shut down the U.S. financial markets for a week.

Omniscient God does not generally inform us of the specifics of the future. Surely He understands that we would not handle it wisely.

Who could have predicted only ten years ago the profound effect that the Internet would have on our businesses, personal lives, and ministries? Even the high-tech devices in the James Bond movies of the 1960s and 1970s pale in comparison to cell phones, GPS units, or worldwide overnight package delivery and tracking.

Major changes not only span decades, they are also recent—painfully recent. Only a few years ago the World Trade Center symbolized our powerful economy. Only a few years ago Enron and MCI WorldCom were hot growth stocks. Only a few years ago an audit by Arthur Andersen meant credibility. This reminds us of the next grip.

GRIP 3: CONVENTIONAL WISDOM IS USUALLY WRONG.

Because of the truth of Grip 2, it stands to reason that many employed economists, financial news network hosts, the pundits, and the gurus will be wrong most of the time. There's an old saying that economists have correctly predicted nine out of the last five recessions. Many economists and analysts receive large salaries, present convincing charts, and use sophisticated financial terms, but still they are wrong more than they are right.

Think back with us to the beginning of 1980. The last year of Jimmy Carter's presidency saw interest rates soaring, high inflation, stagnant American industry, and gold and silver prices hitting new highs. If you had listened to the conventional wisdom of that time, you would have avoided the stock market, kept money in CDs, and put more money in gold and silver.

The result of following conventional wisdom? You would have lost a precious amount in the precious metals markets; they have never come close since that time to the price levels of early 1980. Then you would have missed out on the stock market boom beginning in 1982 while watching your CD yields plummet.

Go back to the early 1970s. The investing rage was the "Nifty Fifty." Investors viewed this group of fifty growth stocks as a "no brainer." You were to buy them and hold them forever because they were sure to go up. They included IBM, Coca-Cola, Avon Products, Xerox, Proctor and Gamble, and other premiere growth companies of that time. As the market started to decline in early 1972, Nifty Fifty mania became even stronger; investors believed the "big giants" were safe.

The result of following conventional wisdom? Soon the stock market declines of 1973–1974 caused the Nifty Fifty to crash. The group of Nifty Fifty underperformed the stock market during the subsequent decades. Many of the companies never regained their share price high of 1972. A number of the companies are no longer around or are in financial trouble today, such as Unisys, Digital Equipment, Polaroid, and Xerox.

If you had gotten your grip on this truth, wouldn't you have been less likely to invest in the Internet craze in the mid-to-late 1990s? Market observers were saying we had entered a permanently high plateau. (If those words strike a familiar note, it is because similar words described the market in the 1920s before the stock market crash.) Analysts in *The Wall Street Journal* predicted the Dow Jones Industrial

Average would hit 36,000 soon.[9] As you may recall, the Dow has not yet reached 12,000. As of the time of this writing, it remains in the 8,000 range.

GRIP 4: NO SINGLE INVESTMENT WORKS ALL THE TIME.

Reminiscent of the Nifty Fifty, most thought the U.S. large-company growth stocks—such as General Electric, Enron, Intel, and Lucent—were the "sure thing" in the 1990s. They had realized eye-popping returns for several consecutive years. To many new investors in the stock market during this time, diversification meant diversifying their investment portfolios among small, midsized, and international growth stocks. They were still 100 percent in the stock market. The potential returns for bonds and money market funds were too low and too boring.

After the stock market peaked in March 2000, large-company stocks were down, bonds were up, and money market returns remained positive. Another case of conventional wisdom being wrong. Evidence that no single investment, or even investment in a particular category, will always work.

Here's a summary of the proof of this grip. The table on the following page shows which type of financial asset provided the best return during each year of the last twenty-six years. You can see that the best-performing asset type regularly varies.

Market Leaders (1977-2002)

Year	U.S. large company stocks	U.S. small company stocks	International stocks	Emerging market stocks	U.S. corporate bonds	Non-U.S. bonds	Savings account
1977						✓	
1978			✓				
1979		✓					
1980		✓					
1981							✓
1982					✓		
1983		✓					
1984					✓		
1985			✓				
1986			✓				
1987						✓	
1988				✓			
1989				✓			
1990						✓	
1991				✓			
1992		✓					
1993				✓			
1994			✓				
1995	✓						
1996	✓						
1997	✓						
1998	✓						
1999				✓			
2000					✓		
2001					✓		
2002						✓	
Number of times market leader	4	4	4	5	4	4	1

After the inflationary 1970s and the farmland boom, Michael decided that farmland would be a wise investment. Land prices were growing faster than inflation. Rather than buy a few acres, he liquidated his other assets to buy Iowa farmland at about $4,000 an acre. His reasoning was that farmland would never go down in value. There was only a limited supply of land, and people would always have to eat. Not only did he sell other assets, but he also borrowed to buy millions of dollars of farmland.

Michael lost his grip. He was wiped out when farmland plummeted in value later in the 1980s. What he didn't anticipate was that crop yields drastically increased with improved cultivation techniques and seed engineering. These improvements caused less land to be needed (Grip 2—uncertainty). The farming economy then experienced a prolonged downturn (Grip 1—markets go up and down) caused by high interest rates, lower prices, and higher costs. The resulting bankruptcies forced more land to be sold at lower and lower prices.

Michael had thought he was making a wise and safe investment, but Grip 4 reminds us that nothing works all the time. Wisdom and experience have taught us not to put all our eggs in one basket.

GRIP 5: CORRECT FINANCIAL PRINCIPLES WORK CORRECTLY THROUGHOUT TIME.

Despite the trend of interest rates, despite the political party in power, despite recent stock market performance, despite the value of the dollar compared to the Japanese yen, the correct financial principles work. Where does one go to find these principles? Ultimately, their source is the Bible. From the rich wisdom of Solomon to the divine teachings of Jesus to the inspired writings of Paul, the Bible's principles remain relevant.

The writers of most secular financial how-to books agree, perhaps unwittingly, with the Bible. When they say to live frugally, avoid credit cards, keep an emergency savings reserve, invest for the long term, give to charity, and make plans, they are stating biblical principles. Truth is practical, effective, and ultimately comes from God. We will discuss these biblical financial principles in chapter 2.

Now that we have discussed these gripping truths, let's apply them. Refer to the summary chart on the following page to help you handle these grips and apply them to your own situation.

low range for the last thirty years. Even though some may not have the ideal job, most willing people can find some type of work.

American productivity increases. Conventional wisdom used to say Americans were too inefficient and that Japan would overtake us economically. Japan has been in a recession for more than a decade, but the U.S. has remained strong. The Internet and use of computer technology have fueled significant productivity increases.

Advanced medical treatments. Increased longevity from medical advancements has extended the lives of many, including me.

Improved financial reporting. The corporate and accounting scandals, though recently a problem, will ultimately help the markets. Corporate management, boards of directors, and accountants will pay more attention to providing accurate, understandable financial information.

Declines in the stock market. Although this may not seem like a positive sign, I believe it is. The decline is effective medicine for speculative fever. Now perhaps people will have reasonable expectations going forward. Maybe they will be more careful with their investing.

Although I still have concerns—such as high levels of consumer debt, increasing trade deficits with other countries, and low rates of giving—there are positive signs.

ASK RON

Q. When you hear the evening news about another down day on Wall Street, how do you keep from getting depressed?

A. I try to make my plans based on principles. Principles last and survive the day-to-day "noise" of the cable financial networks and the evening news.

I also think of a story I heard. One day several friends were discussing their thoughts about life. They each quoted a saying that meant the most to them.

When it came his turn, a man who was known for his wisdom thought a moment. He finally said that his favorite saying was from the Bible: "And it came to pass."

The others were surprised that he had not picked a more famous saying from the Bible, such as "Love thy neighbor as thyself."

He replied, "This is what I try to remember whenever life gets me down. Sometimes I get so caught up in the moment that I forget that things come and go. You have to take the bad with the good and find the faith to keep going."[10]

Ask Yourself

- In what financial areas do I tend to worry more and trust God less?
- What is some conventional wisdom that I am following too closely?
- What are financial lessons that I can learn from others or from history instead of learning them the hard way?
- Who are people in my life whom I can trust for godly counsel?

CHAPTER 2

Planning to Last: The Five Ps of Financial Planning
— OR —
"Do Not Pass Go. Do Not Collect $200"

If we command our wealth, we shall be rich and free; if our wealth commands us, we are poor indeed. We are bought by the enemy with the treasure in our own coffers.
EDMUND BURKE

Every man ought to have money on his mind. No man ought to have money on his heart.
ANONYMOUS

The plans of the diligent lead surely to advantage,
But everyone who is hasty comes surely to poverty.
PROVERBS 21:5

How much better it is to get wisdom than gold!
And to get understanding is to be chosen above silver.
PROVERBS 16:16

A fter years of discussing their desires, Dan and Martha finally reached the time of their retirement. They were leaving the larger city and building their dream home on a lake in North Carolina. They had reviewed house plans, dreamed about the décor, and longed for a deck with a view. They couldn't wait—especially Martha—to have a new, larger home.

Dan had paid his dues and risen from a laborer to a supervisor in his thirty-five-year career at three large manufacturing companies. Martha had worked for retail department stores as an assistant store manager during the last twenty years. They both had dutifully saved in their 401(k) retirement plans offered by their various employers. Their combined retirement plan savings totaled $250,000 at January 1, 2000.

Tallying up the lot, construction costs, and new furniture, Dan and Martha figured the new home would cost $300,000. They wanted plenty of room for any future grandchildren. They preferred not to have a mortgage in retirement. So, to pay for their new home, their approach was to use the proceeds from the sale of their old home for $100,000 and take distributions of $200,000 from their 401(k) plans.

Dan and Martha readily admitted that they were not very sophisticated financially, but their approach made sense to them. To get a second opinion, however, they consulted a local financial planner who advertised in the stock market section of their local newspaper.

The financial planner was a kind and persuasive man who worked for an insurance company. He recommended that they obtain a $200,000 mortgage for their new home instead of using their 401(k) money. He told them they should do what the rich folks do: make money off of other people's money. He said they could earn more in the stock market based on the returns of the recent 1990s than what they would pay in mortgage interest. So he recommended a variable annuity, investing in a variety of stock market investments.

Feeling a bit uneasy about this new approach to their retirement, Dan and Martha also consulted their banker before deciding. He said that they would qualify for a mortgage, his bank would be pleased to lend them the money, and the interest would be tax deductible. In addition, he said now was a good time to borrow. He further added that the low mortgage interest rate of 7 percent could not realistically drop much further.

After these meetings, Dan and Martha decided to take out a mortgage for $200,000. After all, the financial planner and the banker were the "financial experts."

Two years later Dan and Martha were living in their dream home on the lake—but not with the peace and enjoyment they expected. They had underestimated the increase of other costs of a bigger home—higher insurance, utilities, property taxes, alarm system, furnishings, maintenance, and so on.

Also, the local economy dropped when a large regional plant shut down and moved to Mexico. The water levels of the lake behind their home also dropped. A prolonged drought and changes at the dam authority caused lower water levels. This, of course, made the lake less attractive for boating and fishing. These factors lowered housing prices in the area.

To make matters worse, the balance in their variable annuity had dropped substantially during the stock market declines of the early 2000s. After reaching a peak value of $250,000, the variable annuity statement showed a gut-wrenching balance of $110,000, down from the original $200,000. Unfortunately, the balance of their mortgage did not decline like their investment; it was $176,000.

They contacted their financial planner to cash out their variable annuity. They simply could not bear any more potential losses. To add insult to injury, they learned that a surrender charge of 5 percent, or

$5,500, applied. In the fine print they had agreed to pay a surrender or redemption charge if they cashed out of their variable annuity investment within the first seven years.

Sadly, many people have learned hard lessons in fundamental financial principles, perhaps some with circumstances similar to Dan and Martha. The reminders of fundamental financial principles needn't be learned so painfully. Before we delve into specific issues in the remainder of this book, let's review certain basics and see where Dan and Martha erred. We call these financial basics the Five *P*s of Financial Planning.

1. PARADOX OF PROSPERITY

A paradox runs counter to our typical thinking. It is contradictory to what we think is normal. The paradox of prosperity is simply this: the more prosperity attained, the greater potential worry and bondage.

The more things you obtain, the more you have to track them, plan for them, store them, analyze them, insure them, pay tax on them, dust them, discuss them with others, secure them, and bequeath them. When you buy a boat or an RV or a vacation home, consider the time, energy, and money expended. Most of us would feel compelled to use these items regularly, even if inconvenient or not as enjoyable, to get our money's worth.

Dan and Martha's dream of the big house on the lake was really more than they could manage. Instead of less worry, they took on more worries by buying too much too soon.

As we know deep down, our lives consist of more than our stuff. Jesus said, *"Not even when one has an abundance does his life consist of his possessions"* (Luke 12:15). Yet we hold on to a false belief that if we have more possessions, then life will be better, perhaps easier, and even simpler.

After talking to thousands of people over the last twenty-five years, we have realized an interesting correlation: The more money we have, the more we tend to worry about losing it. That fear is not without justification. However, we believe that in many cases it causes poor decision making when it comes to personal finances.

We've also observed that in many cases more money equals less freedom, not more. The logic behind this conclusion is that the more money you have, the more options you have. Consequently, you spend more time and energy making decisions and managing your resources.

2. PERSPECTIVE ON THE ECONOMY AND THE FINANCIAL MARKETS

By using the key grips outlined in chapter 1, you can have the right and proper perspective. In looking back over our country's history, we can easily find events and trends to cause worry about our economy.

The early 1930s. We were struggling with a national depression, an unemployment rate of 25 percent, lack of confidence in the stock market, and bread lines.

The early 1940s. We were at war and had to ration key basic staples, from rubber to gasoline to steel.

The early 1950s. We were worried about the spread of communism and spent money to build bomb shelters in our backyards.

The early 1960s. We feared the Russians' lead in space exploration and held our breath during the Cuban Missile Crisis.

The early 1970s. We experienced an oil crisis, the Vietnam War split the generations, income tax rates were near all-time highs, the President authorized a break-in at the Watergate building, and the federal government placed wage and price controls on the economy.

The early 1980s. We thought Japan would overwhelm us economically, unemployment neared 10 percent, interest rates hit 20 percent, and inflation stayed in the double digits.

The early 1990s. We fought a brief war in the Persian Gulf and experienced a recession after the booming late 1980s.

The early 2000s. We experienced the longest decline in the stock market since the 1930s and endured the terrorist attacks on the World Trade Center and the Pentagon.

This quick review of the decades of our lives and our parents' lives reminds us of the gripping truths of chapter 1. We do not intend to imply a ten-year forecasting model or that bad events only happen at the beginning of a decade. We simply wish to provide a quick overview of economic history for events and times you may remember. These help provide a perspective that our economy and markets are resilient, cyclical, and unpredictable.

Dan and Martha needed to get a grip. They lost their proper perspective. They wrongly assumed the high-flying stock market of the 1990s would continue. They put too much of their net worth in a house whose value dropped when unforeseen conditions occurred. Then, if they tried to sell either their house or their investments, they would have incurred significant loss by buying high and selling low.

Economic uncertainty need not spell disaster or upheaval in your personal finances. Nor should it foster fear when you are living by biblical principles of money management.

3. PRINCIPLES TO LIVE BY

As we mentioned in chapter 1, correct principles work throughout time. They also work for all people and for all types of organizations.

Several years ago, I (Ron) had the opportunity to testify before a Senate subcommittee that was holding hearings on "Solutions for the New Era: Jobs and Families." While others on the panel pressed for more social programs, I said I believed the American family could benefit from following a four-part financial plan:

- Spend less than you earn.
- Avoid the use of debt.
- Maintain liquidity.
- Set long-term goals.

The committee chairman listened carefully and recited the points back to me. He paused a moment, then said, "It seems like this plan is not just for the family. It seems it would work at any level."

"Yes," I laughed, "including the government."

I was smiling, but I did not miss the opportunity to exhort the senators to exercise strong leadership through wise financial planning. These four financial principles are so simple that they may easily be overlooked. Yet they have stood the test of time, having been developed and outlined thousands of years ago in the Old and New Testaments.

In our example, Dan and Martha violated the principle of avoiding debt by taking on a mortgage when they had available funds to purchase the house. Then they increased their risk by investing in the stock market. In essence they borrowed to invest in the stock market.

They did not maintain liquidity, that is, keep their funds available and accessible. They put virtually all of their net worth in their home and in an investment with a high surrender charge. They followed worldly wisdom and its incorrect principles, and they suffered.

4. PLANS TO MAKE IT HAPPEN

As implied in the term *financial planning,* another important *P* is having a plan. Because the financial principles previously mentioned run counter to our culture, a plan is needed. As Hall of Fame football coach Tom Landry said, "Setting a goal is not the main thing. It is deciding how you will go about achieving it and staying with that plan."

Often Christians question whether they should do any planning. We are often asked, "Shouldn't a Christian depend totally on God?" Our response is yes, but that doesn't mean that we are to sit back and do nothing. Our faith requires action.

Planning is essential in any life but especially in the lives of Christians. God is an orderly provider. He expects us, even exhorts us in Scripture, to have an attitude and aptitude of doing our best and planning ahead in our decisions. Our plans should remain flexible because God may redirect our paths.

Dan and Martha had discussed their plans. They did not, however, stick to their wise intuition to avoid debt. They also did not receive wise counsel. After receiving unwise advice, they acted on it without evaluating the counsel they received against biblical principles.

If it is worth planning, then it is worth the effort to write it down. Written goals not only provide visible objectives to work toward, they also provide accountability. Make plans that are compatible with God's will. Don't make financial decisions based on what others are doing. *"Commit your works to the LORD, and your plans will be established"* (Proverbs 16:3).

If you need counsel, be willing to ask for it. Many Christians are willing to help others but are never willing to ask for help themselves. That's just our pride getting in the way. All of us need counsel and advice. Pray together about every decision. Prayer brings God directly into our lives and strengthens our faith so we can trust Him in even greater things.

Many of your written plans will be specific to your individual circumstances: when to change jobs, how much retirement savings to attain, how much to give. But some general guidelines apply to all of us. For example, if you currently have credit card debt, we do not recommend that you invest in the stock market to save for a child's college education. You are not yet ready to invest.

In my (Ron's) investment firm, we use the following plan called "The Concept of Sequential Investing." This plan provides several specific steps you can take to help you become financially stable. These steps, or priorities, taken in sequence, make sense at any income level and under any economic scenario, regardless of your individual financial goals.

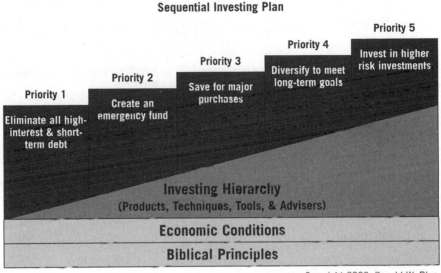

Sequential Investing Plan

Priority 5
Invest in higher risk investments

Priority 4
Diversify to meet long-term goals

Priority 3
Save for major purchases

Priority 2
Create an emergency fund

Priority 1
Eliminate all high-interest & short-term debt

Investing Hierarchy
(Products, Techniques, Tools, & Advisers)

Economic Conditions

Biblical Principles

Priority 1: Eliminate all high-interest debt. The best investment you can make is to get rid of all high-interest, short-term debt. By paying off credit-card balances and automobile or other installment loans, you get a guaranteed return of 15 to 21 percent—money you would otherwise be losing to exorbitant interest charges.

Priority 2: Create an emergency fund. Once you have repaid all high-interest debt, begin funneling your available cash into an interest-bearing checking account or savings account. Keep three to six months' worth of living expenses in this account. Use this fund to meet the cost of minor emergencies, such as car or home repairs, so that you can avoid incurring any additional debt. When you "borrow" from this account, plan to pay back the money as soon as possible.

Major emergencies, from the loss of a job to an unexpected medical crisis, need not spell disaster. If you can stash several months' worth of living expenses in savings, you will have the liquidity you need to ensure your financial survival should a catastrophe occur. These contingency funds will become all the more important if a recession or depression occurs. As John F. Kennedy said, "The time to repair the roof is when the sun is shining."

Priority 3: Save for major purchases in a bank CD or government-security mutual fund. Once you have laid a firm financial foundation in steps 1 through 3, you are ready to pursue conservative, low-risk investments, which are ideal saving vehicles for purchases such as cars, furniture, and even the down payment on a home. How much money you choose to invest depends on your individual needs. Choose investments that mature in five years or less so you can withdraw funds without incurring penalties.

Priority 4: Diversify investments to meet long-term goals. Investing for long-term goals—such as a college education, increased giving, or financial independence—calls for a diversified investment portfolio. Mutual funds, real estate, bonds, and international equities may all be part of your picture. At this point you may wish to consult a qualified financial adviser who understands your needs and goals, as well as your personal tolerance for risk. Interview several prospective advisers and choose someone you trust to make objective recommendations.

Priority 5: Invest in higher risk and higher return investments. Investing in hard assets, venture capital, and the like carries a significant amount of risk. It also demands time and a willingness to become actively involved with the investments themselves. This type of investing isn't for everyone, but if you are going to pursue this step, be certain that you have completed the first five steps in the sequential strategy.

No one can predict the future, but following these sequential steps can provide peace of mind in the present and also as you pursue long-term goals.

5. PARADIGM OF BELIEF

This is where the rubber meets the road. The resulting actions and decisions ultimately reveal what a person believes about God and His Word. You either believe Him and follow His way, or you decide your way is better. Note that God has a much better track record than any of us.

We like the way Henry Blackaby describes this pivotal point: "The crisis of belief is a turning point where you must make a decision. You must decide what you believe about God. . . . How you live your life is a testimony of what you believe about God."[1]

In the next chapter we will examine an effective approach to making sound financial decisions.

ASK LARRY

Q. Is it a sin, or is it wrong, for Christians to borrow money?

A. Benjamin Franklin's *Poor Richard's Almanac* quotes, "Neither a borrower nor a lender be." Although it's good common sense, it's not from God's Word. However, many Christians feel that all borrowing is prohibited according to Romans 13:8, *"Owe nothing to anyone except to love one another; for he who loves his neighbor has fulfilled the law."* In order to interpret this Scripture properly, it must be considered in light of the context in which it appears. In this particular reference, I do not believe Paul was talking specifically about money; he was teaching that we are never to allow someone to do something for us if we are not willing to do even more for him or her.

Neither borrowing nor lending is prohibited in Scripture, but firm guidelines are given. Borrowing is discouraged, and, in fact, every biblical reference to it is negative. Consider Proverbs 22:7: *"The rich rules over the poor, and the borrower becomes the lender's slave."* The scriptural guideline for borrowing is clear. When you borrow, you promise to repay. Literally, borrowing is making a vow. God requires that we keep our vows, so be sure to pay what you owe (see Psalm 37:21).

Scripture shows us that we are to be cautious about borrowing, and it should never be normal. Yet, when you look at our society, you find that borrowing is rampant. Americans think it is normal to borrow for periods of thirty to forty years. We have created an economy that borrows to exist. That is not God's way. God's Word says that borrowing is a consequence of ignoring His statutes and commandments (see Deuteronomy 28:43–45). It is never God's best for His people.

ASK RON

Q. Where in your sequential concept of investing does a person invest in 401(k) and Roth IRAs?

A. At times, you may need to see the steps we recommended as a balanced approach rather than focusing only on sequential. Some steps may overlap. Let's use the 401(k) as an example. If your company provides a matching contribution (such as putting in fifty cents for every dollar you invest), then you should take advantage of that. Participate in the plan to obtain the match even before you pay off some of your debt, such as cars, home equity, etc.

If you have high-interest credit card debt or department store revolving credit at 18 to 24 percent, you should pay that off as quickly as possible. Perhaps even before participating in the 401(k)-matching plan.

If there is no matching, then it becomes a different decision. If there's no matching by your employer, then I would typically stay in the sequence of paying off your nonmortgage debt and saving outside of your retirement plan to build an emergency fund. The liquidity is important. Then you can begin putting money into the retirement plan or IRAs because of their tax benefits.

ASK YOURSELF

- What financial principle am I prone to violate?
- What are my short-term goals?
- What long-term financial goals should I write down and discuss with my spouse?
- Have my investment steps gotten out of sequence?

THE DECISION-MAKING PROCESS
— OR —
"I Am Not Sure If I Am Decisive or Not"

Sometimes I lie awake at night, and I ask, "Where have I gone wrong?"
Then a voice says to me, "This is going to take more than one night."
CHARLIE BROWN, *PEANUTS* [CHARLES SCHULZ]

When a person with experience meets a person with money, the person
with experience will get the money. And the person with the money
will get some experience.
UNKNOWN

So then do not be foolish, but understand what the will of the Lord is.
EPHESIANS 5:17

Trust in the LORD with all your heart,
And do not lean on your own understanding.
In all your ways acknowledge Him,
And He will make your paths straight.
PROVERBS 3:5–6

A s we enter the latter part of our lives, we are faced with more critical financial decisions. Often these decisions come in rapid succession within a few weeks or months of one another.

Consider the following situations:

- Bob's employer offers an incentive plan for early retirement. He has two weeks to decide if he will retire, what lifetime payout options to choose for his pension, how he will rollover and invest his 401(k), and what health insurance coverage to obtain for his family.

- Carol, age sixty-two, is recently widowed after her husband's sudden heart attack. She has decisions about whether to retire herself, how to invest life insurance proceeds, whether to begin withdrawals from his Roth IRA, which health insurance option to choose, and which Social Security option to choose.

- Harold, age seventy and a half, receives the following letters in the same week: a letter from his financial adviser about required distributions from his IRA, a proposal for long-term care insurance, and a large certificate of deposit needing renewal.

Is it any wonder we are more anxious (some may say "grumpy")? Is it any wonder we find more wrinkles and gray hair as we get older?

These financial decisions are stressful because they often have many zeros after them. They are once-in-a-lifetime—or irrevocable. They involve complex products and technical information. The terms alone can make your head spin: joint-survivor pension payout option with ten-year certain period, single-premium immediate annuities, supplemental-Medigap-COBRA health insurance, required minimum distributions from IRAs.

Perhaps even more stressful to many is that the success or failure of these decisions involves factors beyond our control. The first uncontrollable and unknowable factor is the future direction of our economy, as we discussed in chapter 1. The second is our longevity. How much easier our financial decisions would be if we knew when we would die and when we would face serious illness. The Bible says, *"It is appointed for men to die"* (Hebrews 9:27). But God chooses not to tell us the time of our appointment.

Analysts and researchers refer to the set of financial choices involving longevity and the economy as the "Impossible Decision." It is impossible to know when you will die. Therefore, it is impossible to know the best decision in terms of dollars. For example, it is impossible to know for sure the payout option from your pension plan that will give you the most money over a period of time. You can know the best possible decision only after it is too late.

For people who are more prone to desire control and certainty in their lives, the Impossible Decision may cause despair. For those who do not have a personal intimate relationship with the omniscient, omnipotent living God, the implications of the Impossible Decision may leave them hopeless.

For Christians who have a vibrant personal relationship with Almighty God, the Impossible Decision provides another opportunity to place their faith and trust in God. Although the unknowable realities of the Impossible Decision apply to Christians, we have an additional Counselor in the Holy Spirit, additional insight through prayer and other believers in the church, and wisdom from God's Word.

Throughout the remainder of this book, we will discuss specific financial issues and decisions. First, however, we wanted to provide help with the process of making financial decisions. The key topics in this chapter include the following:

1. What is wealth? If I want my wealth to last a lifetime, what exactly is it that must last?

2. How do I find God's will for financial decisions? If He knows how many (or how few!) hairs are on my head, He must know and care about my bank balance.

3. What obstacles interfere with good decision making?

WHAT IS WEALTH?

Past civilizations show that wealth has often been based on the number of cattle or camels owned, land possessed, oil deposits, and many other material possessions. In the early economy of the United States, wealth was related to how much land one owned. Later, wealth related to resources, such as gold or silver or other natural elements in the earth. Then, during the Industrial Revolution it related to how much one had accumulated in worldly goods—namely, money.

In today's economy, wealth is still related to money, but there are other measures of wealth. Professionals, such as doctors, attorneys, dentists, and others, are thought to be "wealthy" because of their income-earning potential.

For example, a doctor coming right out of residency is capable of borrowing great amounts of money to go into business without any collateral other than his education. What is his credit based on? His potential productivity. Therefore, even the talents and the abilities you have are part of your wealth, as is your credit or borrowing ability.

Another interesting view of wealth comes from Buckminster Fuller. Mr. Fuller was an architect by trade, but some say he was also a mad scientist. In his patent application for a geodesic dome, he described the true nature of wealth. He described it as a person's ability to survive a certain number of days forward. In other words, if you stopped working today, how long could you survive?

Robert Kiyosaki, author of the best-seller *Rich Dad, Poor Dad,* does a good job of distinguishing between net worth and wealth. Net worth, the difference between the value of your assets and liabilities, consists of a person's expensive junk in his or her garage and opinions of what things are worth. "Wealth measures how much money your money is making and, therefore, your survivability."[1]

True wealth also extends beyond the financial and quantitative to the spiritual and qualitative. A missionary had been invited by a church pastor to bring a message one Sunday morning. The missionary had one married son and five married daughters, all of whom were active in Christian work and present at that service. His five daughters had just finished singing a special song before the congregation.

As he rose to speak, a friend whispered, "Emil, you are a wealthy man." The missionary didn't have much money, yet his friend considered him wealthy. Emil's friend was correct. He was truly wealthy. His trust was in God, and so was his children's.

Some Christians are wealthy in the riches of this world, but their conceit and trust in money have robbed them of their spiritual wealth. Your spiritual wealth is more than just possessions and money. It is all of God's blessings: abundant life here on earth, eternal life in heaven, family, friends, health, peace, marriage, spiritual gifts, fruits of the spirit, and much more. *"Instruct those who are rich in this present world not to be conceited or to fix their hope on the uncertainty of riches, but on God, who richly supplies us with all things to enjoy"* (1 Timothy 6:17).

HOW DO I FIND GOD'S WILL FOR FINANCIAL DECISIONS?

In answering radio listeners' or clients' questions about God's will for their financial decisions, we remind them that no one has perfect insight into God's will—especially perfect insight for another person. Usually a decision requires wisdom from God's Word, the counsel of godly people, and personal discernment in order to determine God's will for our lives. Too many Christians make decisions based on the "open door" philosophy: if God does not block it, it must be OK. Unfortunately, Satan can also open doors, many of which lead to elevator shafts.

Financial decisions by their very nature will involve numbers. The first step is "running the numbers." Jesus alluded to this in His teaching that any wise person "counts the cost" before building a house. This is called due diligence—doing some figuring, making a spreadsheet, or scratching numbers on your pad. Although it may seem obvious, it amazes us how people sometimes forget the obvious of checking the numbers. A little bit of math helps common sense rise against emotion.

Beyond the practical number crunching, every decision must meet at least two criteria for a Christian. First, it must be compatible with God's Word. Some decisions are objective enough to be eliminated on the basis of direct contradiction to God's Word. God will not lead you into a business that will cause you to violate His principles of finance.

For example, Joe had a history of poor financial decisions. Although he made a good income, his family lived an expensive lifestyle. So they lived paycheck to paycheck for many years, causing anxiety for Joe's wife.

Joe's company offered an early retirement incentive program to him at age fifty-five. Rather than take the pension option to receive a monthly income for the rest of his life and his wife's life, he chose the lump-sum payout. He took the lump sum and borrowed additional money to open a restaurant. He rejected health insurance coverage offered through work because his monthly budget could not afford the premiums.

Joe's decisions may not be compatible with God's principles. He likely is putting his family at risk. Joe might say that he is trying to provide, but his decisions are questionable. *"If anyone does not provide for his own, and especially for those of his household, he has denied the faith, and is worse than an unbeliever"* (1 Timothy 5:8).

God warns about debt throughout the Bible. It is not His approach to lead you into a situation in which you would incur a large debt through borrowing. Many times people believe God is leading them into an area, and He may be, but they lunge forward without getting His day-to-day direction or without following what He has already clearly spoken.

The second criteria you must have is a peace and a personal conviction "before God." The Bible says, *"The faith which you have, have as your own conviction before God. Happy is he who does not condemn himself in what he approves"* (Romans 14:22). You are held to the highest standard, which requires constant input from the Holy Spirit to keep your direction straight. It means you are accountable if you defile your conscience by doing something you believe is wrong. This belief must be based on a firm conviction from God.

Even with the best discernment, it is possible to do things that are out of God's will. The key is not to let pride get in the way but to admit it when you are wrong and then go in a new direction.

Should you consult with anyone else to make sure you are in sync with God's Word and have the right convictions? Certainly so. Remember that *"without consultation, plans are frustrated, but with many counselors they succeed"* (Proverbs 15:22). This doesn't mean you run your life based only on what others think, like a weak politician making policy by the latest polls. But use those people God has placed around you as a resource. Be accountable to them.

WHERE DO I TURN FOR ADVICE?

Spouse. One of the best sources of counsel is a Christian spouse. By God's design, husbands and wives tend to balance each other with their strengths and weaknesses, insight and oversight, and risk tolerances and reward motivations. For example, women are often more conservative in financial matters, such as investing or taking on debt, than men. We have observed more examples than we can count of men ignoring the opinion of their wives and later regretting it. *"House and wealth are an inheritance from fathers, but a prudent wife is from the LORD"* (Proverbs 19:14).

Adult children. If your children are mature adults, then they have a unique vantage point about your strengths, weaknesses, and desires. They understand the immediate and extended family dynamics. They love you and want the best for you.

Keep in mind that you are not asking their permission but seeking their counsel. It is especially important to seek their counsel if they have a professional background or knowledge base that you do not have. We have been amazed at the parents who do not consult their son, the attorney, about their own legal matters. Or they don't consult their daughter, the human resources and benefits manager, about pension options.

Why? Sometimes parents are stubborn, unteachable, and prideful. Sometimes they fear their children will "know too much" about the parents' finances. Sometimes, more innocently, they find it hard to think of little Susie or little Johnny as capable, competent professional adults. These are poor excuses not to seek the counsel of adults. Parents might as well get some direct benefit from helping their children get all that education from kindergarten to college!

Church members. If you are active in your local church, you have fellow believers with similar values to consult. The disadvantage of using only your spouse and children for counsel is that they may have a present or future vested interest in your decision. That vested interest may be emotional or financial, so broaden your circle of "counselors" to your church.

Too often people listen to the advice of superficial acquaintances, such as hairdressers, occasional golfing buddies, or neighbors. Instead, have lunch with your pastor, elder or deacon, Bible study leader, or your prayer partner. These are people to use as a sounding board to let you know if you are biblically on track.

Professionals. Professionals have the advantage of technical expertise and objectivity. Your family and church friends love you and may be prone to please you. This may affect their objectivity. Consult a lawyer or a certified public accountant. Their experience with other clients going through similar decisions can help you. They can warn you of pitfalls and provide alternatives you missed.

At the same time, recognize that certain professionals may have their objectivity colored if they sell products you are contemplating. For example, if you ask an insurance agent whether you should buy a certain type of insurance or you consult a banker about whether to get a loan, then you can guess a bias toward their likely response. If all they have is a hammer, then everything begins to look like a nail!

WHAT ARE THE OBSTACLES TO GOOD DECISION MAKING?

Fear. As financial counselors, we have observed that people wrestle with two primary fears: the fear of failure and the fear of the future. It is not sinful or wrong to experience fear, doubt, or uncertainty. Neither is it uncommon. Moreover, Christians are not immune to fear.

The first step to overcoming fear is to admit it. Be aware of it and how it can affect your decisions. One or more of the following questions may characterize fear-based decisions.

- Are my decisions made quickly, with little forethought?
- Are my decisions presumptive? Are they based on conclusions that have little or no substantiating proof?
- Have I taken ill-advised counsel? Have I made decisions under the counsel of untested, unreliable, or biased sources?
- Do I experience anxiety or tension about my decisions?

By contrast, wise and thoughtful decisions are usually characterized by a sense of stability and calm. Scripture attests to this pattern. *"And the peace of God, which surpasses all comprehension, will guard your hearts and your minds in Christ Jesus"* (Philippians 4:7). Good decisions, financial and otherwise, are marked by peace not panic.

Analysis paralysis. Whether it is from fear or from our personalities, another obstacle to good decision making is indecisiveness. It is possible to overanalyze so that you never make a decision at all. But by making no decision, you really are making a decision.

Let us explain further. William James, an early pioneer in psychology, described "Life's Living Option." Suppose you're in a vehicle stalled on a railroad track and a powerful train is headed toward you.

1. You have a choice to make: you can stay in the car and try to get it started. Or you get out of your vehicle to seek safety.

2. Assume you have the ability to make that choice.

3. There is a consequence to your choice: life, if you get out; certain death if you stay in and are unable to start the car.

4. But while you are deciding, you are in one of the choices. You are in the vehicle. The longer you stay, deciding your options, the more limited your options become.[2]

Let's connect this concept to your financial decisions. You are debating whether to invest more in the stock market while it is lower than the previous year or keep it in an interest-bearing account. Interest rates are low, so you don't like the low earnings from the bank account. You think it may be a good time to invest, but you wonder if the market may go even lower. Your analysis could continue for months. But while trying to decide, you have already decided. The result is that you chose the interest-bearing account by default.

If you have a problem being decisive, consider these five steps to greater decisiveness from the *Executive Leadership* newsletter.

• Carefully consider all the facts and options.

• Pay attention to your gut.

• Once you make a decision, don't second-guess yourself.

• Act, knowing that you'll probably make more good choices than bad ones.

- Anticipate success, but don't be afraid to fail. Ask: "What will happen if I don't act? And if I do?"[3]

Financial temptations. We each have our own financial temptations. For some, it is houses and furnishings. Others care little about their houses but can blow it on cars or clothing. Others spend too much on recreation.

Succumbing to financial temptations can undermine good financial decisions. As someone once said, "If you really want to do something, you will find a way. If you don't, you will find an excuse." Knowing your weaknesses and being accountable to others can help you resist temptation.

Most financial temptation comes at us from well-meaning people. The dealer who sells RVs or boats is not engaging in deceit or sinful activity in trying to sell the latest model.

But other financial temptations come from those who perpetuate fraud and lies. The cold call about an investment offering a "guaranteed" 12-percent return is too good to be true. The business opportunity advertisement offering high income for part-time work at home is a temptation often offered with evil intent. The e-mail from Nigeria offering 30 percent of $20 million to help move money out of the country is a scam.

The Bible observed this phenomenon many years ago. *"But those who want to get rich fall into temptation and a snare and many foolish and harmful desires which plunge men into ruin and destruction"* (1 Timothy 6:9). The Bible cautions us with this advice, *"Therefore be careful how you walk, not as unwise men, but as wise, making the most of your time, because the days are evil"* (Ephesians 5:15–16).

To implement this biblical advice, here are some practical suggestions from the U.S. Postal Inspection Service to guard against mail fraud.

- You should never have to pay to receive a prize or enter a sweepstakes contest. If payment is required, it's illegal.

- If you're told you're guaranteed to win a prize, or no risk is involved, be skeptical.

- Any lottery that involves a foreign country and is conducted through the mail is illegal.

- Legitimate charities don't ask for donations in conjunction with a contest. The problem is that many phony charities use names that sound or look like respected organizations.

- Don't give Social Security, credit card, or bank account numbers or other financial information to callers you don't know. If it's a reputable group, this information won't be requested.

- Don't be pressured into making an immediate decision. Get all information in writing before agreeing to enter a contest, make a purchase, or give a donation. If you suspect fraud, contact the Postal Inspection Service.

- At the homes of elderly friends or relatives, look for stacks of unsolicited mail proclaiming the recipient to be "a guaranteed winner" or offering lottery tickets for sale.

- Watch for an unusual number of packages arriving for the elderly containing inexpensive costume jewelry, plastic cameras, or wristwatches.

- Note if the elderly are receiving unsolicited telephone calls from fast-talking operators offering "fantastic" opportunities to claim prizes or make surefire investments. If so, you can arrange for unlisted phone numbers for them.

- Volunteer to help balance checkbooks of the elderly and ask about questionable checks or sudden, large withdrawals.

- Offer to pick up the mail of seniors to see if they are receiving unsolicited sweepstakes or lottery offers. If so, they may be on a variety of "sucker lists" circulated by con artists.

We will end this chapter with a summary of the principles of financial decision making that will apply to the specific issues throughout the remainder of this book. One of your more challenging decisions will be about retirement. We will focus on retirement issues in the following chapter.

---

10 PRINCIPLES OF FINANCIAL DECISION MAKING

1. Evaluate your motives (Psalm 139:23–24).
2. Run the numbers and keep your finances current (Luke 14:28–29).
3. Consider your witness (1 Thessalonians 5:22).
4. Avoid "get-rich-quick" mentality (Proverbs 28:22).
5. Give to the needs of others (2 Corinthians 9:13).
6. Never co-sign a loan or act as surety (Proverbs 6:1–5).
7. Avoid indulgence (1 Timothy 6:7–8).
8. Prepare for decreases (Philippians 4:12–13).
9. Seek godly counsel (Proverbs 11:14).
10. Seek God's peace (Proverbs 10:22).

ASK RON

Q. What is a financial decision that you have made in the past and are still benefiting from today?

A. To pay cash for cars. After I decided to pay cash for all cars, related decisions followed to help my financial position. We kept cars longer. We bought less expensive cars because we didn't have enough saved for the luxury cars. Avoiding debt to buy an item that rapidly depreciates in value is one of the best decisions I made.

Finishing a close second was our decision to pay off our mortgage. That was, and is, such a sense of freedom.

Yet Christ has granted you a position of value and importance because of His love. When we let these truths become real in our lives, we can let go of the fear of failure and the fear of making wrong decisions. His love and grace remain even when we do make decisions that, in retrospect, were not the best.

ASK YOURSELF

- In what ways am I wealthy, in the fullest meaning of that word?
- Do I give myself permission to be open to new possibilities?
- Whom have I been omitting from my "consulting team"?
- What decision am I facing, or will soon be facing, to which I can apply the ten principles of financial decision-making?
- Regarding a decision I am currently facing . . .
  - What is the worst that can happen if I do (or do not do) this?
  - How likely is the worst-case scenario to occur?
  - How likely is the best-case scenario to occur?
  - Am I willing to live with the consequences, favorable or not, of this decision?

CHAPTER 4

RETIRING CONVENTIONAL WISDOM ABOUT RETIREMENT

— OR —

"A Retirement Is a Terrible Thing to Waste"

If you want to make God laugh, then tell him your future plans.
WOODY ALLEN

I can't get old; I'm working. I was old when I was twenty-one and out of work.
GEORGE BURNS

I hate the word *retirement*.
JOHNNY CARSON

The chiefest action for a person of spirit is never to be out of action; the soul was never put in the body to stand still.
JOHN WEBSTER

"A little sleep, a little slumber,
A little folding of the hands to rest,"
Then your poverty will come as a robber
And your want like an armed man.
PROVERBS 24:33–34

M r. Cathy had owned and operated a successful local restaurant called the Dwarf House in Georgia for more than twenty years. Nearing fifty, he was at the age when many begin contemplating retirement. Perhaps selling out, or at least slowing down. Maybe moving to Florida. Instead he kept working. He even opened another restaurant with a new concept. Located in a mall, offering only chicken, and closed on Sundays, the first Chick-fil-A began in 1967.

Now headed by its eighty-two-year-old chairman, Truett Cathy, Chick-fil-A is one of the largest privately owned restaurant chains in the U.S. With more than a thousand locations, Chick-fil-A passed the one billion-dollar sales mark in 2000.[1]

Truett Cathy could retire in ease, but he continues to work forty-hour weeks. A recent article in the *Atlanta Business Chronicle* noted that Cathy could make a fortune if he made a public stock offering for Chick-fil-A, but he refuses to consider it. The *Chronicle* quoted him as saying, "We're able to do a lot of things that we wouldn't if we were a public company. . . . And I like to tell people that if we went public I'd be afraid I'd lose my job."[2]

The official company web site states the company's values:

Yet, from the beginning, the first priority for Truett and Chick-fil-A has never been just to serve chicken. It's to serve a higher calling. Our official statement of corporate purpose says that we exist "to glorify God by being a faithful steward of all that is entrusted to us and to have a positive influence on all who come in contact with Chick-fil-A."[3]

More than simply writing a noble statement, Mr. Cathy's company implements this purpose uniquely in the modern business world. Chick-fil-A closes all of its restaurants on Sundays for employees to worship, spend time with their families, and rest. For its kids' meals, Chick-fil-A uses audiocassettes or activities emphasizing character traits such as gratitude or obedience rather than a trinket for an upcoming Hollywood movie.

Mr. Cathy has often said, "It's easier to build boys and girls than to mend men and women." He has taught the same Sunday school class for thirteen-year-old boys for forty-seven years. He started a foster home system, WinShape Homes, to provide long-term family care to disadvantaged children through twelve homes. He began Camp WinShape for children to have a positive youth summer experience. His WinShape Foundation partnered with Berry College to provide spiritual and educational opportunities.[4]

Chick-fil-A began its leadership scholarship program in 1973 to encourage its restaurant employees to further their education. It became the only one of its kind offered by a quick-service restaurant chain. According to the Council for Aid to Education, no other company in terms of size does as much in the scholarship area as does Chick-fil-A. The company has awarded $16.5 million in scholarships to date through thousand-dollar scholarships available to all restaurant employees to the college of their choice.

Past eighty and still using his business skills as a platform, Cathy spoke to congressmen about successful businesses using honest and biblical principles during the congressional hearings about other corrupt businesses. He has appeared on NBC and CNN, participated in the President's Economic Forum, and spoken at Billy Graham's crusade.[5] Quite an impact for someone who simply describes himself as a good short-order cook!

Truett Cathy enjoys recreation, especially with his motorcycles and vintage antique cars. But he says, "Learn to love your work, and you'll never have to 'work' again."

Born in the same year in the same town as Truett Cathy was Mr. Darton. Mr. Darton was a purchasing agent in a power plant. Throughout his work career he kept a ten-year calendar in his desk drawer in which he X-ed off the days until his retirement date at sixty.

At the water cooler, in the lunchroom, at the retirement parties of his older colleagues, he talked about how he couldn't wait for retirement. He was going to catch up on projects, work in the yard and garden, travel, and golf.

If forced to admit it, Mr. Darton enjoyed many aspects of his job—the people, the mental stimulation, the occasional conferences out of town, the benefits. But, like many of his coworkers and those retiring before him, he daydreamed about getting out and being free. His wife encouraged him to keep working and privately worried if he would run out of things to do after he retired.

After a few months into his retirement, Mr. Darton had finished all the "honey-do" projects around the house. They seemed to be endless when he was working, but now he had to find new things to do.

His church offered several volunteer positions of service to Mr. Darton, but he declined. His standard reply was, "I'm retired now. I have a lot of things I want to do. Besides, we hope to do some traveling."

The travel soon subsided after the first few years. He found it was rather expensive to go on extra trips. After all, they were on a fixed income now. And, quite honestly, it was a little harder living on the reduced income than he had thought it was going to be. Anyway, his wife didn't like being gone too much from their grandchildren and her aging mother. Golf became less interesting after a year of regular playing. It too was expensive.

After five years of retirement, Mr. Darton had seen all the TV he wanted, read all the books he wanted, kept his yard perfect, and was very bored. Still healthy and mentally sharp, he had considered "doing some consulting" to increase his income and help his budget. But he was a bit proud that he was retired and didn't want it to appear that he couldn't make it on his own. Besides, no consulting opportunities came along.

Turning seventy, his ten years of retirement had evolved into a routine of reading the paper for an hour, having coffee with old coworkers, and griping with them about his pension and the cost of prescription drugs. The highlight of his day was getting the mail; the highlight of his week was mowing the lawn.

The annual physical at eighty revealed that Mr. Darton had no life-threatening problems. Other than a little arthritis and a few cancerous skin spots from sun exposure, his doctor said he was in great shape and would likely live several more years. *Ho-hum*, Mr. Darton thought to himself. *I can't imagine several more years like the last twenty years.* Twenty years of monotony. Twenty years of anxiety about his fixed income and dwindling assets.

The stress of higher utility bills and the bondage of a fixed income make it easier for Mr. Darton to yell at the paper boy when the newspaper is a few feet off the driveway. Worry about Social Security and boredom make it easier to curse the neighbor's kids who blow dandelions that might spread to his green, weedless yard.

While riding his lawn mower, he now daydreams about his career years. He was active, felt he was contributing, enjoyed the camaraderie, and certainly enjoyed a higher standard of living. Why did he so look forward to retirement?

Mr. Darton's experience is typical. Compare and contrast the difference between Mr. Cathy and Mr. Darton. Same age, same good health, same good mind, and same faith. Mr. Cathy, a contributor to the economy, a benefactor to society, a supporter of God's Kingdom, an enthusiastic liver of life in his community. Mr. Darton, a dissatisfied retiree, an occasional grouch, a dependent on Social Security, a neutral or even negative presence in his community.

Mr. Darton is not alone. He is more the norm and Mr. Cathy the exception. If many are like Mr. Darton, then we as a society have problems awaiting us in the future, and we as the church are reducing our impact on the world around us.

What's our solution? We are not waiting until the end of the chapter or building to a punchline. It is a four-letter word: W-O-R-K. Keep working. Change careers and begin another. Work as a volunteer or work for pay. Work part-time. Work full-time intermittently at various jobs. Work in the winter, play golf and fish in the summer. Get attuned to the idea of continuing to work.

We see advertisements and magazines glamorizing retirement. The travel industry, the financial services industry, and homebuilders in the Sunbelt states all dangle the retirement utopia to encourage sales of their products. The social chatter among those fifty and over frequently includes phrases of "I can't wait until retirement."

How did we get to this point in America? Is retirement biblical? What are alternatives to the typical views of retirement?

A BRIEF BACKGROUND OF AMERICANS' VIEW OF RETIREMENT

The American view of retirement is a relatively new idea, an invention of an affluent society. For our great-grandparents, there was no such thing as retirement. People continued to work as long as they were able to or as they needed to. They worked on the farm or worked in the smokestack factories of a newly industrialized society. They likely worked until they died. Or, when they became unable to work, they moved in with their adult children or extended family who probably lived on the family farm or in the same town.

America experienced significant changes from 1900 to the 1930s.

These changes laid the foundation for a populist movement demanding government-provided pensions.

Industrial revolution. Working people changed from self-employed agricultural and tradesmen into wage earners for larger manufacturing companies. Workers then had less economic security; their security could be threatened by factors outside their control, such as recessions, layoffs, or bankrupt businesses.

Urbanization. Workers moved away from farms and extended family to the cities where the jobs were.

Few employer retirement plans. Only 2 percent of the nation's workers were covered by any employer pension or retirement plan.

Increased life expectancy. From 1900 to 1930, average life spans increased more rapidly than at any other time in recorded history: ten years.[6]

These trends, combined with the ongoing Great Depression, provided the political pressure to pass the Social Security Act of 1935. Signed into law by President Franklin D. Roosevelt, the Act provided for benefits to be paid to workers at age sixty-five. How was this age chosen?

A common myth is that the U.S. chose age sixty-five because Germany, the first nation in the world to adopt an old-age social insurance program, used age sixty-five as the starting point for benefits. Initially, Germany used an age of seventy for retirement age in 1889 but later lowered it to age sixty-five in 1917.

The U.S. committee drafting the benefit rules for Social Security noted two sources for selecting age sixty-five. One practical, and politically justifiable, source was the age used in other pension programs at the time. Most of the few private pensions used age sixty-five. Of the various state old-age pension systems, about half used age sixty-five and half used age seventy. The federal Railroad Retirement System passed a year before by Congress used age sixty-five.

Second, the committee used actuarial studies to see if expected benefit payments using age sixty-five would result in a manageable system with modest payroll taxes. The actuarial studies confirmed that, based on the assumptions, age sixty-five was sustainable.[7]

So our current idea of retiring at age sixty-five is based on an arbitrary selection! Age sixty-five is not a medically determined point when a person can no longer meaningfully function. Age sixty-five passed the actuarial muster because the average life expectancy at birth in 1930 was fifty-eight for men and sixty-two for women.[8]

Americans quickly adopted this view of retiring at sixty-five with the government footing the bill. And why not? At the time the jobs were backbreaking, dangerous, or monotonous. If you asked a steel furnace worker or an assembly line worker if he enjoyed his work, he would have thought you were crazy. Generally, work was not viewed as meaningful or purposeful. Men and women struggled to buy their next meal or clothe their children. They worked to survive.

Why not retire? People didn't expect to live very long after sixty-five. Unemployment rates were historically high. Society needed to open up positions in the job market for many young people. The Social Security system appeared strong, with far more workers paying payroll taxes than people receiving benefits.

Through various amendments to the Social Security Act occurring over time, Congress added the optional age of sixty-two, began Medicare coverage for those aged sixty-five, and provided cost-of-living increases. As the U.S. enjoyed more prosperity and leisure time through an expanding economy in the 1950s and 1960s, Americans began to view retirement as an entitlement.

Many now see retirement as a normal right and a normal rite of passage. Early retirement has even become something of a status symbol. When people say that they "were able to retire" at fifty-five or sixty, they seem to relish the fact with pride. Perhaps others do envy them. But the times are a-changin'.

CURRENT RETIREMENT TRENDS

The past trends that formed Americans' initial belief about retirement are no longer predominantly true today. Yet people are retiring earlier and earlier! Here are the key trends, many opposite of earlier trends, affecting retirement today.

Changing nature of work. Work has moved from primarily physical and manual to mental and information based. Although stress may exist, most jobs do not require as much physical stamina. Many people in their sixties and seventies have the stamina to perform the service and information-oriented jobs of our economy.

Work is more fulfilling and meaningful than in the past. Computers, machines, and automation have removed much tediousness. Famed management professor and author Peter Drucker (who, by the way, continues consulting, teaching, and writing at age ninety-two) states:

> Today, a growing number of people find . . . that they enjoy their work, that they become better as they become older, that they are not ready to retire even though they may have the means to do so. A large and growing number of people—I call them "knowledge workers"—not only do much better financially than anybody in history has ever done, they do infinitely better in terms of personal fulfillment.[9]

Longevity. After hearing of an acquaintance dying suddenly at age sixty, haven't you said something like, "My! That's young!" Your great-grandparents would rarely have uttered such a remark. Increased life spans are a reality and are trending even longer. This trend of living longer is overwhelming retirement planning for the Social Security system and for individual decision making. For Americans the life expectancy at birth in 2000 is 76.9 years. But if you had already made it to age sixty-five, then men could expect to live until eighty-two and women until eighty-four.[10] Remember, this is "on average." Many will live beyond this age. If you take early retirement at sixty, you may spend twenty-five years or more in retirement.

Changing needs of employers. Unemployment has remained low for the last twenty years. The primary human resource problem for many employers, especially in the services and retail industry, is finding enough workers.

To save overhead and be more flexible, companies are using more part-time workers, consultants, or temporary workers. Retirees desiring more leisure time and flexibility are well suited for temporary positions. Many employers have also realized that older workers are more dependable, have a better work ethic, are more honest, and have more valuable life experience to draw upon than younger workers. Unlike the 1930s, employers now have a demand for older workers.

Lower interest income and a declining stock market. With yields on certificates of deposits hovering between 2 and 3 percent in the early 2000s, it is difficult to "live off the interest." The lower interest rates help borrowers—mainly younger families buying houses, cars, and college education on credit. The lower interest rates hurt savers—mainly retirees with money in the bank and no debt.

The stock market decline in the early 2000s also eroded the asset bases of many retirees. The current trend is to return to work to supplement their lower income and prevent further erosion of their invested assets.

IS RETIREMENT SCRIPTURAL?

There is only one reference to retirement in the Bible: Numbers 8:25. It says the priests of the Tent of Meeting (later the Temple) should retire from that function at the age of fifty.

So apparently retirement was not common to God's people, even during New Testament times. It could be argued that people didn't live as long back then, which is generally true. But they did live long well into Abraham's day, and yet retirement wasn't mentioned.

The underlying premises of Americans being entitled to retirement are not biblical.

- Leisure is more valuable than work.
- Older people are less useful and less productive.
- At an arbitrary age, one can withdraw from responsibilities to enjoy the comfortable rewards from past labors.

These premises contradict the following sample of verses about the value of work.

Whatever you do, do your work heartily, as for the Lord rather than for men. (Colossians 3:23)

Do you see a man skilled in his work?
He will stand before kings;
He will not stand before obscure men. (Proverbs 22:29)

And to make it your ambition to lead a quiet life and attend to your own business and work with your hands, just as we commanded you, so that you will behave properly toward outsiders and not be in any need. (1 Thessalonians 4:11–12)

"Let your light shine before men in such a way that they may see your good works, and glorify your Father who is in heaven." (Matthew 5:16)

"I have coveted no one's silver or gold or clothes. You yourselves know that these hands ministered to my own needs and to the men who were with me. In everything I showed you that by working hard

in this manner you must help the weak and remember the words of the Lord Jesus, that He Himself said, 'It is more blessed to give than to receive.'" (Acts 20:33–35)

Even when we were with you, we used to give you this order: if anyone will not work, then he is not to eat, either (2 Thessalonians 3:10)

Arise and work, and may the LORD *be with you* (1 Chronicles 22:16)

He who tills his land will have plenty of food,
But he who follows empty pursuits will have poverty in plenty.
(Proverbs 28:19)

You yourselves know how you ought to follow our example, because we did not act in an undisciplined manner among you, nor did we eat anyone's bread without paying for it, but with labor and hardship we kept working night and day so that we might not be a burden to any of you. (2 Thessalonians 3:7–8)

A brief review of biblical characters shows that many heroes of the faith are remembered by achievements in their latter years. Leaving out the extreme ages of those living during the era of Genesis, such as Noah and Abraham, we find many active "seniors":

Moses confronted Pharaoh and led the children of Israel from Egypt at age 80 (Exodus 7:7). He served as judge and CEO of the Israelites from age 80 until his death at 120 (Deuteronomy 34:7).

Aaron accompanied Moses and served as his spokesman from age 83 to age 123 (Numbers 33:39).

Joshua, the successor to Moses, led the nation of Israel until his death at 110 (Joshua 24:29).

Zacharias and Elizabeth, described as "advanced in years" (Luke 1:7), conceived and took on the task of parenting John the Baptist.

Anna—How did this widowed prophetess spend her time at age eighty-four? Luke 2:36–37 says she *never* left the temple, serving night and day with fastings and prayers. She prayed over and spoke about Jesus when He was a baby.

John the disciple—Many scholars estimate he was nearing ninety when exiled at Patmos for preaching about Jesus. While there, he received and wrote Revelation.

Many of the apostles did their greatest work after the time we would have considered them to be old men. When Paul admonished Timothy not to let anybody mock him because of his youth, Timothy was older than forty at the time.

We find inspiration in modern-day heroes of their faith as well. Billy Graham, barely able to walk from Parkinson's disease, recently held a crusade in Dallas, Texas, at age eighty-three. His organizers called it one of their most successful crusades: "In all, more than 255,000 came to the four-day event with about 12,000 making commitments to Christ."[11]

Mother Teresa of Calcutta served the blind, the aged, lepers, the disabled, and the dying in India until her death at age eighty-seven.

Bill Bright, founder and president of Campus Crusade International, calls this time of his life his most productive and prolific in writing. At eighty-one, he continues to serve as chairman of Campus Crusade but spends most of his time writing books and preparing training materials— all while hooked up to an oxygen tank due to his pulmonary fibrosis condition, an ailment affecting the lungs.

In addition to these followers of Christ, consider the noteworthy accomplishments of other men and women in their latter years as shown on the following pages.

ACCOMPLISHMENTS OF PEOPLE 59½* AND OLDER

Age

59 **Michaelangelo** painted "The Last Judgment" on the ceiling of the Sistine Chapel.

60 **P. T. Barnum** produced his first circus.

60 **Albert Einstein,** a German scientist who left for the U.S. after Hitler came to power, wrote a personal letter convincing President Roosevelt to develop atomic bombs before the Nazis. Einstein's last published work was at age seventy-one.

65 **Bear Bryant** ran the Crimson Tide as football coach at the University of Alabama.

66 **Colonel Harlan Sanders** started the Kentucky Fried Chicken chain.

69 **Ronald Reagan** was elected to his first term as president and was the oldest person to be elected president (until he was reelected at seventy-three).

70 **Sam Walton** continued as president and CEO of Wal-Mart. Remained chairman until his death at seventy-four.

71 **Winston Churchill** was the British prime minister who played an instrumental role in rallying support not to give in to Hitler. Became prime minister again at age seventy-seven and served another four years.

71 **Golda Meir** became prime minister of Israel.

73 **Picasso** completed some of his greatest works and continued to paint until age ninety.

75 **Nelson Mandela** became the first black president of South Africa after being a political prisoner for twenty-seven years.

Age

76 **Grandma Moses** started to paint because her arthritic fingers could no longer embroider.

77 **Eleanor Roosevelt** was appointed U.S. delegate to the United Nations.

81 **Benjamin Franklin** was elected as a delegate to the U.S. Constitutional Convention.

83 **Thomas Edison** signed his last patent application (total patents received during his lifetime was 1,093).

84 **Paul Harvey** awakes before sunrise to record his daily radio broadcasts heard all over the world.

87 **Bob Hope** entertained American troops in the Persian Gulf.

88 **Frank Lloyd Wright** completed the famous Guggenheim Museum.

88 **Fenya Crown** completed a 26.2-mile marathon race, her eighth.

91 **Milton Friedman,** Nobel Prize winner of economics for his economic theories, continues writing articles, advising presidents informally, making speeches, and serving as senior research fellow at the Hoover Institution.

100 **Strom Thurmond** completed his eighth term as a U.S. senator.

* Note: The beginning date for penalty-free withdrawals from Individual Retirement Accounts—yet another arbitrary age conjured up in legislation but having no relationship to productivity.

To put it in the right balance, it would seem clear that, biblically speaking, God's norm is for us to stay active all of our years. So, at best, retirement is a transition to a different vocation—not a lapse into dormancy. Most people obviously can't keep the same pace at sixty-five that they did at twenty-five or forty-five, but there is much they can do. Therefore we recommend a new retirement paradigm.

NEW RETIREMENT PARADIGM

We recommend viewing retirement as an adventure-filled next phase of life. Expect to work and seek meaningful work. We agree with Peter Drucker, who says, "Reaching retirement age no longer means reaching the end of your working life."[12]

Even if God has blessed you with adequate resources so that you need never work again, why waste your talents?

While in their fifties, Steve and Patty sold their successful business for top dollar to a multinational corporation. They ended their first phase of work but moved to other meaningful challenges. He used his leadership abilities, without pay, to serve as an administrator at his church. She served on the board of a women's abuse shelter.

They enjoyed the rewards of their labor with plenty of golf, bridge, and travel to visit grandchildren; but he also served on the board of trustees for a seminary and an international missionary organization. Steve and Patty combined their personal travel with work for the missionary organization (out of their own pocket) to visit and encourage many missionaries.

Jesus contrasted those who use their talents well, like Steve and Patty, and those who don't in a story recorded in the Bible:

> *"For it is just like a man about to go on a journey, who called his own slaves and entrusted his possessions to them. To one he gave*

five talents, to another, two, and to another, one, each according to his own ability; and he went on his journey.

"*Immediately the one who had received the five talents went and traded with them, and gained five more talents. In the same manner the one who had received the two talents gained two more. But he who received the one talent went away, and dug a hole in the ground and hid his master's money.*

"*Now after a long time the master of those slaves came and settled accounts with them. The one who had received the five talents came up and brought five more talents, saying, 'Master, you entrusted five talents to me. See, I have gained five more talents.'*

"*His master said to him, 'Well done, good and faithful slave. You were faithful with a few things, I will put you in charge of many things; enter into the joy of your master.'*

"*Also the one who had received the two talents came up and said, 'Master, you entrusted two talents to me. See, I have gained two more talents.' His master said to him, 'Well done, good and faithful slave. You were faithful with a few things, I will put you in charge of many things; enter into the joy of your master.'*

"*And the one also who had received the one talent came up and said, 'Master, I knew you to be a hard man, reaping where you did not sow and gathering where you scattered no seed. And I was afraid, and went away and hid your talent in the ground. See, you have what is yours.'*

"*But his master answered and said to him, 'You wicked, lazy slave, you knew that I reap where I did not sow and gather where I scattered no seed. Then you ought to have put my money in the bank, and on my arrival I would have received my money back with interest. Therefore take away the talent from him, and give it to the one who has the ten talents.'*

"For to everyone who has, more shall be given, and he will have an abundance; but from the one who does not have, even what he does have shall be taken away." (Matthew 25:14–29)

In the culture of this story, the word *talent* means coinage, or monetary units. Some conclude then that the primary application of this parable of the talents is investing in higher-return and higher-risk investments rather than burying money. While investment lessons may be a secondary application, Jesus mainly emphasized the need to expend effort, to take on challenges, and to maximize resources for the benefit of the kingdom of God.

If you desire to quit what you've been doing and do something else, that's fine. If you have enough money to be able to quit, that's great. Praise the Lord for that. But then volunteer with a charity, try a short-term foreign mission trip, help your church, or work with kids in your community.

It seems to us that many people simply plan to quit, to just park it at sixty-two or sixty-five and not do anything else productive. We know many people, and certainly you do too, who have done that. We believe they are going to be accountable to the Lord. Many have made enough money to stop working; they can afford to quit and play all the time. They are not doing anything useful for God or others. They tip God to keep Him off their back, but they are not effective for Kingdom purposes.

Many, however, are living out this new retirement paradigm. May these few examples inspire your creativity as God leads you to where you can join Him during or before retirement.

- Dave, a former water utility employee, travels the world in his retirement. He tests and treats water in Third-World countries with various missionary organizations during short-term mission projects.

- Anne retired as a registered nurse at fifty-five. She takes on various temporary nurse positions in U.S. cities where nurses are in short supply. Working half the time as her old job, Anne makes almost as much as before. In between assignments she has time to devote to her passion: mentoring young girls and teaching them abstinence through local crisis pregnancy centers.
- Matt sold his environmental consulting firm to enter seminary. By taking occasional consulting jobs, he paid for his seminary tuition, kept his skills up-to-date, and was able to accept a lower-paying position at a struggling inner-city church.
- Linda, a former management professor, works with her church's state organization to assist churches with growth plans, strategy planning, and human resource issues.
- Tom didn't get much of a chance to work with his hands as an accountant, but he always loved working with tools. After retiring the first time, he now works at Home Depot, works with tools, helps others learn about them, receives health insurance, and gets off work at 1 P.M. daily to care for his aged parents.
- Grant, a retired pastor of forty years, lends his experience to small churches as an interim pastor. In between pastoral positions he serves as a volunteer chaplain at a federal Job Corps Center. In a small town he ministers to hundreds of young people from all over the nation as they try to learn life skills many miles from their homes.

Other organizations, charities, seminaries, and churches offer resources to help those over fifty plug in to the next phase of life and service. An example is the Finishers Project (www.finishers.org). It acts as a missions matchmaker of individuals to various mission organizations. Aimed at baby boomers, the Finishers Project provides a free service of matching potential volunteers' user profiles, gifts questionnaire, and travel preferences to the needs of more than eighty Christian organizations. It is not a sending agency but links your skills and desires to organizations looking for more people resources.

Bob Buford, chairman of Buford Television, Inc., helped to bring attention to the tremendous resources and potential of those who wish to move "beyond success to significance" in his book *Halftime*. He wrote, "God has a wonderful plan for the second half of your life: to allow you to serve him by doing what you like to do and what you are good at."

Why does this new retirement paradigm of seeking and finding fulfilling work make sense?

1. It fits the models and principles of the Bible.
2. It provides a solution, or at least a partial solution, to the challenge of making your wealth last. Think financially with us for a moment. Accountants define an asset as something of value that helps produce income. If it does not produce income now or in the future, then by definition it is not an asset. The most valuable asset for most people is their ability to earn an income. Let's say that Jane's pleasant personality and energy make her an easy selection for a greeter at Wal-Mart. She is able to earn $9,000 a year working part-time. That is an asset. Let's compare to another asset. At an interest rate of 3 percent, she would require $300,000 in a CD to earn $9,000 a year. Or, it usually takes at least three or four lower-income residential rental properties to earn $9,000 a year.
3. It helps your overall well-being. Harvard University conducted a study of older people and their happiness. This study, which lasted sixty years, found that older workers do better in life by picking work that allows them to be creative, to play, and to make younger friends. These factors can be more important to late-life happiness than income (if basic needs are met).[13]

4. It contributes to others, to society, and even to the kingdom of God.

5. It is easy to do because opportunities and jobs are plentiful. Have you tried to find a contractor or repairman recently? If you were fortunate enough to have found one, you learned from their bill that they can earn a decent living. That reminds us of a story we heard.

A fellow had an overflowing toilet causing flooding in his house. He called his handyman friends and regular plumber but no one was available. He finally found an ad in the Yellow Pages: "Emergency plumbing service, available on demand."

The homeowner called the plumber in the ad. The plumber came and took about three minutes to find a little toy that a child had flushed down the toilet. He retrieved the toy and successfully flushed the toilet. The overflow subsided and the homeowner asked him how much he owed the plumber.

The plumber replied rather matter-of-factly, "$150."

"One hundred fifty dollars! Goodness sake, you haven't been here five minutes. I'm a doctor and I don't make $150 for five minutes."

The plumber replied, "I didn't either when I was a doctor."

Several biblical principles can be applied to your vocational choices. Each person is uniquely designed by God (see Psalm 139:13–14). Each person has been given unique talents for a purpose (see Romans 12:6–8). Each person must develop those talents for excellence (see Proverbs 22:29). And work is a stage for a person's higher calling (see Matthew 5:16).

ARE WE ALONE IN OUR RECOMMENDATION?

After rereading what we have just written about our views and the biblical views of retirement, we realized that this might be a tough pill to swallow. As Malcomb Forbes said, "Advice: It's more fun to give than to receive." After all, our views fly in the face of what many have come to believe about retirement. Some may say that we Bible-quoting financial teachers are spoiling the party and popping the balloon of retirement utopia.

We researched what secular financial experts, authors, and researchers believe. We did not aim to validate or change our opinions but to see how radical we were. Interestingly, we found that almost all agree with us!

Particularly striking to us is that the titling and marketing of most retirement books are aimed to appeal to most people's daydreamish view of retirement. But the contents of these books describe the reality. We found a disconnect between the titles and the recommendations.

Retire Rich: The Baby Boomer's Guide to a Secure Future

"What would be so bad about working ten or twenty hours a week at a job we enjoy in order to supplement our retirement income?"

(by Bambi Holzer, John Wiley & Sons, 1998)

The Complete Idiot's Guide to Retiring Early

Early on, the authors note on page 5 of a 341-page book about retiring early:

"Income from part-time work in retirement for several years may make a big difference in how comfortable your retirement will be. Add the satisfaction gained from your efforts and the companionship of co-workers, and it doesn't sound so bad."

(by Dee Lee, certified financial planner, and Jim Flewelling, Alpha Books, 2001)

Die Broke: A Radical Four-Part Financial Plan to Restore Your Confidence, Increase Your Net Worth, and Afford You the Lifestyle of Your Dreams

"Forget about retirement. Believe me, giving up this living death is actually an empowering act that opens up undreamed-of opportunities for your personal, professional, and financial growth."

(by Stephen Pollan, attorney and certified financial planner, and Mark Levine, Harper Business Books, 1997)

The Die Broke Complete Book of Money

"I'm 71, and frankly, the prospect of not going to the office each day seems totally absurd to me. I believe work is good, not only for the pocketbook but for the mind and the spirit. It provides you with a purpose. The end of one career can be the springboard for entry into another. You may find that, when it comes to quality of life, you agree with me that the best retirement is no retirement at all."

(by Stephen Pollan, attorney and certified financial planner, and Mark Levine, Harper Business Books, 2000)

Retiring Right—2002 Edition

The author, Lawrence J. Kaplan (who, by the way, is age eighty-seven), calls his first chapter "Working in Retirement."

(Square One Publishers, 2002)

Making the Most of Your Money

"To retire early . . . you need a job. Forget about 'early retirement' in its classic, freeboating sense. Think about earning enough money to fill the gap between your pension income and your expenses so you can leave your capital alone to grow."

(by Jane Bryant Quinn, Simon & Shuster, 1991 and 1997)

BUT WE ARE NOT SAYING . . .

We believe strongly that Americans and the American economy are better off if we reject our typical view of retirement. But we are not saying that all retirement is wrong or bad. Many must retire for health or disability reasons. That is certainly understandable.

Many retire to take care of aging parents or a dying spouse or to become parents again as grandparents. Others are forced to retire because of mandatory age limits in certain professions or companies, or because of layoffs. Some may desire a type of "sabbatical" retirement for a year or so. Often, however, people in these cases may return to the workforce after a period of time or may begin new careers or volunteer efforts.

Neither do we believe that planning for retirement is wrong. God declares that we should save something for the future. That may include saving for purchases or, ultimately, retirement. *"There is precious treasure and oil in the dwelling of the wise, but a foolish man swallows it up"* (Proverbs 21:20).

We would not want any readers to misinterpret our opinion to imply that work is the most important activity in life. Certainly, many people— especially men—have put too much of a priority on their work to the neglect of their relationship with Christ, their families, and their overall balance in life. We do not advocate a workaholic approach.

We are simply saying that if a Christian has a good, full life and enjoys what he does, he will be useful throughout his entire life, not just in his early years. God may have more in mind for your retirement years than you have imagined possible. To be prepared for all the possibilities He has in store for you, you will need to secure income sources. Your living expenses will continue, so you need income to last. Our next chapter will help you review and maintain your income.

ASK LARRY

Q. I am putting all that I can in my retirement savings. Is it wrong to plan for retirement by saving in a 401(k) or IRA?

A. No, it's not wrong. Either a 401(k), a traditional IRA, or a Roth IRA are excellent tax-advantaged ways to save. I have saved using IRA accounts.

I do have a concern though. Some in America have developed a mania about retirement savings and the necessity for storing large amounts of assets. People often save 10 to 15 percent of their income in a retirement plan but then say that they cannot afford to give 10 percent to God's work.

Some think they need to retire with a vast amount of assets and then spend much more than they did during their working years. That is not true. Once you set a pattern for living, it will not change substantially after retirement, except in many cases it may go down. If you have learned to adjust your standard of living during the working years, then retirement will be a comfortable adjustment. The Christian who hoards money to be used for retirement is being deceived.

There is nothing wrong with saving in moderation for retirement. But there is something wrong with storing unnecessarily, believing that is the only way to provide for later years. Whatever its guise, living for retirement and hoarding is the wrong approach.

Reassess your attitudes as a Christian. Are you really worried that if you don't store now you will have to do without later? Do you believe that God is capable of supplying in your old age, or is your faith a myth?

This pressure to have enough resources to begin and sustain retirement lifestyles results in stress, worry, and an earthly focus rather than a Kingdom focus.

ASK RON

Q. In this chapter you did not advocate retirement, yet your firm likely makes a good portion of its investment fees from clients investing for retirement. How do you explain that apparent contradiction?

A. Our firm does earn fees from investments within retirement plans and IRAs. In this chapter we emphasized continuing to serve, continuing to volunteer, continuing to work. How will a person fund those endeavors? By saving and investing for that phase of life.

To echo what Larry touched upon, saving for retirement and hoarding for retirement are two different things. Some people save and invest for retirement excessively and hoard. If we had a client that we perceived was motivated by fear resulting in hoarding, we would like to think our relationship with him would allow us to challenge him on his philosophy and attitude. The attitude is the root of this difference between planning and hoarding.

ASK LARRY

Q. What should I do if my company does not provide a retirement plan?

A. It is difficult—nearly impossible—to live comfortably on Social Security benefits alone. If your company does not provide a retirement plan, you should begin an independent retirement plan, such as a traditional or Roth IRA, for both you and your spouse. In addition, you need to concentrate on becoming debt free by the time you feel you need to retire.

ASK RON

Q. What are your personal plans for retirement?

A. I prefer to call it "rehirement" rather than retirement. I have no plans to retire. Vocationally, I may do different things and try different options, but I do not see myself retiring from my purpose in life. My purpose is to help fulfill the Great Commission. I don't retire from that. I just may help fulfill it in different ways.

ASK LARRY

Q. What are your personal plans for retirement?

A. I love to play golf, but fortunately God has given me a golf regulator. Since I had my left shoulder blade removed, I can play no more than once per week. With my tongue firmly planted in my cheek, I say, if God restores my shoulder, then I'll believe He wants me to play more often.

Seriously, I don't plan to retire. I want to write or teach or speak for as long as I can. We all have a relatively short time on this earth and a long time in eternity. My retirement will come in eternity; I trust yours will too. Foremost in your retirement planning, then, should be the prospect of standing before the Lord and giving an account for the way you have handled your life and your money.

Because of my cancer and related treatments over the past eight years, I see retirement almost from a totally different perspective now. I have been forced to slow down. I am still involved with Crown Financial Ministries and the daily radio programs, but I can't run the organization on a daily basis anymore. I am not trying to get out of working, just trying to pace myself for a longer period of time. More of us should view retirement as a sustainable slowdown instead of a work stoppage.

ASK YOURSELF

- When I think of retirement, what are my feelings and emotions?
- Am I interested more in what I can get from society or pleasure or what I can contribute to God's Kingdom?
- What are my reasons for retirement?

- In light of the parable of the talents, are my planned activities likely to receive praise or a rebuke from my Master?
- Whom have I known who did not handle his or her retirement period wisely? What reasons contributed to the poor use of retirement?
- What person comes to mind who would receive praise from his or her Master for the use of retirement?
- What will I desire from my job in later years besides income?
- What would my ideal job or volunteer activity in retirement be?
- What fields or subjects would I most enjoy learning about?

CHAPTER 5

INCOME TO LAST
— OR —
"Money > Month = Relief"

I have enough money to last me the rest of my life,
unless I buy something.
JACKIE MASON

Money frees you from doing things you dislike. Since I dislike doing
nearly everything, money is handy.
GROUCHO MARX

Annual income twenty pounds, annual expenditure nineteen six, result
happiness. Annual income twenty pounds, annual expenditure twenty
pound and six, result misery.
CHARLES DICKENS, *DAVID COPPERFIELD*, 1849

It is the blessing of the LORD that makes rich,
And He adds no sorrow to it.
PROVERBS 10:22

T hank you, good ol' GM." Sue's dad repeated that phrase every month when he saw his pension check in the mail.

Sue's mother carried on his tradition after he passed away. Her parents primarily lived on that "good ol' GM" monthly pension check plus a little Social Security. Those checks lasted their entire lives.

In her dad's time, workers spent most of their careers at one company. In return for the lifetime of service, the company provided a pension that paid a monthly benefit for life. That won't be the case for Sue and her husband. Neither of their employers offers pension benefits; they offer 401(k) plans. Besides, Sue and her husband have each worked at three different companies during their careers.

Sue's generation encounters different trends: companies reducing or eliminating traditional pensions, workers changing employers more requently, companies shifting the investment responsibility to employees, and workers and spouses living longer after retirement.

As you age and transition to new phases of life, you will still need an income stream. The financial planning issues change from the accumulation of assets, the emphasis from the ages of the twenties to the fifties, to converting assets to income. From a recent study the following is a breakdown of the sources of income for elderly people.[1] Keep in mind that these are not necessarily recommended percentages but actual percentages of the existing elderly population:

Social Security	38 percent
Earnings from work	21 percent
Pensions and retirements plans	19 percent
Income from investments and assets	20 percent
Other (family assistance, gifts)	2 percent

In this chapter we will examine these major sources of income and consider ways to make them last.

SOCIAL SECURITY

We have observed that your wealth will not last if you place too much of your dependence on Social Security. Consider the words of the top-ranking official of the Social Security Administration on the front page of every benefits statement sent to every working American:

> But Social Security can't do it all. Social Security was not intended to be the sole source of income when you retire. You'll also need a pension, savings, or investments. Think of Social Security as a foundation on which to build your financial future.
>
> JO ANNE B. BARNHART, COMMISSIONER, SOCIAL SECURITY ADMINISTRATION
> IN YOUR SOCIAL SECURITY STATEMENT

For a brief background, each person who has earned forty credits during his or her lifetime is eligible to receive Social Security benefits. You can earn up to four credits per year if you work and earn income of $890 per quarter. The number of credits and your earnings during your work history determine the amount of your Social Security benefit.[2] Each year the Social Security Administration sends "Your Social Security Statement" letter showing your earnings record and estimated benefits. (By the way, it is a good idea to review this closely for any errors.)

The final determining factor in the amount of your benefits is when you begin receiving your benefits. You may start early at age sixty-two and receive reduced benefits. You can wait until your "full retirement age" to receive normal benefits. Or you may delay retirement and receive higher benefits. Full retirement age is defined by law. It used to be age sixty-five. But because of the strains on the Social Security system, Congress raised the normal retirement age gradually for those born after 1938.

Year of Birth	Full Retirement Age
1937 (or earlier)	65
1938	65 and 2 months
1939	65 and 4 months
1940	65 and 6 months
1941	65 and 8 months
1942	65 and 10 months
1943–1954	66
1955	66 and 2 months
1956	66 and 4 months
1957	66 and 6 months
1958	66 and 8 months
1959	66 and 10 months
1960	67

For a general idea of typical benefits, the Social Security Administration estimates the following as the average monthly benefits for the year 2003. If you earned higher than average wages throughout your working career, then your benefits would be higher than those shown below as the estimated average benefit per month:

All retired workers	$ 895
Aged couple, both receiving benefits	$1,483
Aged widow(er) alone	$ 862

The maximum monthly benefit may be lower than you think. The maximum depends on the age at which a worker chooses to retire. The maximum amounts for 2003 range from $1,404 for a person retiring at age sixty-two to $2,045 for a person retiring at age seventy.[3] These are based on earnings at the maximum taxable amount for every year after age twenty-one. Whether you earned $100,000 or $1,000,000 every year, your monthly benefit would remain the same.

Although our discussion, as do most analyses of Social Security, focuses on the three key reference ages of sixty-two, full retirement age, and seventy, you can begin benefits at any point in between these ages. For example, if you wait until age sixty-three, then your monthly benefit is higher than at age sixty-two. If your full retirement age is sixty-six and you begin benefits early, your normal, full-retirement age benefits will be reduced as follows:

25 percent reduction at age sixty-two
20 percent reduction at age sixty-three
13 1/3 percent reduction at age sixty-four
6 2/3 percent reduction at age sixty-five

You may decide to continue working beyond your full retirement age without choosing to receive benefits. If so, your benefit will be increased by a certain percentage for each month you don't receive benefits between your full retirement age and age seventy. This table shows the rate your benefits increase if you delay retiring.

Year of Birth	Yearly Increase Rate
1929–1930	4.5%
1931–1932	5%
1933–1934	5.5%
1935–1936	6%
1937–1938	6.5%
1939–1940	7%
1941–1942	7.5%
1943–or later	8%

Each working person in America will have an Impossible Decision (see our discussion about this concept in chapter 3) to consider: when to begin Social Security retirement benefits. Let's use Carol's Social Security information as an example.

Information from Carol's *Your Social Security Statement*

Retirement benefit at age 62	$ 822 a month
Benefit at full retirement age	
(65 years, 10 months)	$1,097 a month
Benefit at age 70	$1,581 a month

Let's review a few other facts and limits that make the beginning point of Social Security such an important and complex decision.

1. Once Carol makes her decision, it is irrevocable. She cannot change it based on her health, her employment, or a change in her finances.

2. Once Carol chooses her age, her monthly benefit remains the same (except for minor cost-of-living adjustments). If she chooses to begin at sixty-two, her benefit is permanently lower. It does not increase to the full retirement amount after she reaches sixty-five years, ten months.

3. If Carol chooses the early retirement age at sixty-two, then she is limited on the earnings she can have each year until full retirement age. The maximum annual earnings without an additional reduction of benefits is $11,520 (2003 limit).

4. When Carol dies, the benefits stop. It is not like a 401(k) where she may have an amount remaining after death. If she waits until age seventy to begin benefits and then dies at age seventy-one, that's it. The government keeps all the money she paid in, but never collected, to pay someone else's benefits. (Separate rules apply to survivor's benefits.) On the other hand, as long as Carol lives, she will receive benefits.

    As an interesting historical note to the lifetime stream of benefits, Ida May Fuller, a legal secretary in Vermont, was the first person ever to begin receiving monthly Social Security benefits. She retired at sixty-five in 1940 after working and paying in taxes for three years. She lived to be one hundred years old! She collected monthly checks for thirty-five years after only paying in for three years. (We suppose the first recipient should have warned policy makers of the ultimate dangers of promising lifetime benefits without an initial funding.)

What should Carol do? Well, it would be easy if she knew when she would die. Not knowing that answer, let's begin by running some numbers. It's possible to compute the break-even point in months and years. In other words, if you choose the normal benefit, how long must you live to have received more benefits than starting early.

In Carol's case her break-even point is approximately 11.5 years. This means that she would have to live to at least 11.5 years beyond her full retirement age of sixty-five years and ten months (or until she was seventy-six years and four months) to come out ahead with the full-retirement age option instead of the early benefit option.

The formula is the following:

(T x E) / D = Number of monthly payments to break even, where . . .

T = Time in months from start of early benefit to start of later benefit
E = Earlier benefit amount
L = Later benefit amount
D = Difference in waiting, or L - E

To see how we arrived at this, consider the following:

T = 46 months (age 62 to age 65, 10 months)
E = $822
L = $1,097
D = $275 (1,097—822)

T x E = 46 x $822 = $37,812 (the amount of benefits between 62
    and 65 yrs. 10 months)
$37,812/$275 = approx. 137 payments
137 / 12 months = 11.5 years

(This formula is an approximation of the break-even point. An even more accurate formula would include the time value, or present value, of the monthly stream of payments. But we know that reading pages of formulas may cause you to put this book down!)

The time period to break even varies depending on an individual's specific circumstances and benefit amounts. When we have completed this calculation for others, the time span usually ranges from eight to fourteen years. Also, remember that a portion of your Social Security benefits may be taxed depending upon the amounts of your other earned and investment income.

Does it seem reasonable that you could live another eight to fourteen years beyond full retirement age? Although you may not know your appointed time to die, you may be able to make a reasonable guess. For example, if you are lean, healthy, and have several immediate family members still alive in their eighties, you may consider waiting until full retirement age benefits or perhaps delaying benefits. Using a different scenario, let's assume the men in your family have all died in their early sixties of heart disease. You are a man taking medication for high blood pressure and cholesterol and can't get rid of that "spare tire" around your waist. We are not doctors, but your life expectancy is probably shorter than average. Then consider starting benefits early, not waiting until full retirement age. But keep in mind, there's a catch to starting Social Security at sixty-two.

The well-publicized future problems of the Social Security system have made many people nervous. We have often written and spoken about this coming actuarial challenge of so many baby boomers retiring and leaving fewer workers to pay into Social Security. This uncertainty has resulted in many taking the attitude of "get my benefits while I can."

We do not think that this uncertainty should drive your present decision making. If you are nearing retirement age, your Social Security benefits are fairly secure. It's your children and grandchildren who should not count on Social Security in its present form.

The main problem, or the big catch, about beginning Social Security *before* your full retirement age is the limit on earned income. If you earn through wages or self-employment income more than the annual limit ($11,520 in 2003, adjusted annually), then your Social Security benefits are reduced. Not simply taxed, not reduced in some date in the future, but your benefits are cut immediately.

For every two dollars you earn above the annual limit, then your benefits are cut by one dollar. Some call it the "two-for-one" rule. This results in a powerful incentive to quit or reduce work for pay. If you take the early benefits, then you lock up your options for several years. If the dream job comes along or your side business starts booming, then you have shot yourself in the foot. Your benefits are already reduced for your lifetime by starting early. Then they are reduced even further because you earned more than the limit. After reaching full retirement age, you can earn an unlimited amount without any reduction in benefits.

This "two-for-one" rule also provides a powerful incentive to cheat the system. We exhort you to reject the temptation to cheat and not report income. Some people drawing Social Security before full retirement age work for cash and never report their wages. Although we acknowledge that many people appear to escape notice, we recommend doing what is right in God's eyes and honestly reporting income. *"He who walks in integrity walks securely, but he who perverts his ways will be found out"* (Proverbs 10:9).

Given the freedom of options, the higher benefit for life, longevity trends, and our retirement paradigm, we generally recommend waiting until full retirement age for beginning Social Security.

We used the hedging phrase "generally recommend" for a reason. There are situations in which starting Social Security early makes sense.

Let's say that you take us up on our challenge in chapter 4 of a new view of retirement, and you wish to volunteer for charity or go on mission trips. Starting Social Security may provide you with the liquidity you need to meet your expenses. The earned income limits would not likely be a problem because you would not have much earned income as a volunteer.

Although we certainly want you to avoid dishonesty, you may be able to plan wisely (and legally) your sources of income. If you are able to control your income, particularly for self-employed people, you may be able to start benefits early by reducing or delaying your earned income.

A good example is a farmer who plans to continue his farming activities well past age sixty-five. He could begin Social Security early and realize a stable income perhaps for the first time in his life. A farmer can delay his income (store crops or build a herd) and increase his expenses in the short term. He may purchase farm machinery or build a needed barn or buy another farm. Then he would have greater depreciation expense that would lower his earned income. After several years of lower income, his farming operations are poised to realize greater earned income. If he is past full retirement age, then he is free from any income limits. Be sure to work with a certified public accountant to help you with the ins and outs of this type of tax and Social Security planning.

Keep in mind that only your earned income is limited. No limits exist for unearned income, such as investment income, pension income, rental income, or IRA distributions.

As we close this discussion on Social Security, remember an advantage to Social Security benefits is that they will continue throughout your entire life. Assuming that the system remains intact and that the annual increases keep up with inflation, then you will not outlive this source of income.

Work—The Little Job Worth $161,000

Stewart and Howard are nearly identical in their situations. Both are sixty-two and retired from the same company. Each has annual living expenses of $30,000 with pension and Social Security income of $20,000. Each has savings of $200,000. Because they have not read chapter 6 of this book yet, both keep their savings in a CD at the local bank.

At the current rate of 3 percent interest, the CDs yield $6,000 per year. So both Stewart and Howard have a shortfall in income compared to their living expenses by $4,000 per year ($26,000 in total income vs. $30,000 in expenses). Neither desires to lower his expenses.

Here's where they begin to differ. Howard does not want to work again. Whether it is pride, laziness, or lack of imagination, Howard opts to tap into his savings rather than work. So he pulls $4,000 per year from his CD principal to meet his living expenses.

Stewart has always been a sports fan. Although he can't run and play as he once did, he loves being around the athletes, the games, and the people. So he works part-time in the summer as an umpire for the local baseball leagues. In the winter he passes out programs at college basketball games. With both summer and winter jobs, he makes only about $7,000 a year. But he loves the air of excitement at the games. He and his wife love the flexibility to travel to visit his grandchildren. And the best part for Stewart? Free admission to the ball games.

From a financial perspective this small amount of part-time work puts Stewart in a significantly better financial position.

Remaining Balance in Their Bank CDs

	After 10 Years	After 20 Years
Stewart	$223,000	$254,000
Howard	$154,000	$ 93,000
Difference	$ 69,000	$161,000

Because Howard was using up principal each year, there was less remaining principal to earn interest. When he earned less interest, he had to pull out more principal to meet his living expenses. This downward spiral accelerates—the power of compounding reversed. After twenty years, Howard faces the prospect of dwindling assets. Being older, he has a more difficult time having the stamina to work and finding opportunities to work.

Stewart, on the other hand, experiences the benefits of compounding interest. He has even more money earning him money. After twenty years of doing something he enjoyed, he could stop and have enough money to last. He is $161,000 better off than Howard. With Stewart's asset base expanded, his withdrawal rate would be much less than Howard's earlier withdrawal rate.

Our combined observation is that over the years most people who do well financially earned their money doing what they did best and what they enjoyed. This observation doesn't end once you reach some arbitrary age of 59½, 62, or 65.

PENSIVE REFLECTION ABOUT PENSION PLANS

The story of Sue's dad that we used to begin this chapter is an illustration of a defined benefit pension plan. This type of plan is where a company defines the benefit, usually based on a formula of years worked and earnings, to be received by the employee. The company sets aside company funds and takes the investment risk to have enough money to pay the monthly pension.

Most large, well-established companies have these defined benefit pension plans as part of their benefit packages. However, the trend among companies during the last ten to fifteen years has been to move away from these plans because of their expense, risk, and complexity to the company. Companies now structure more of their retirement plans toward a defined contribution plan, such as a 401(k), where the contribution is defined but the future benefit is unknown. The employee assumes the investment risk.

Despite the current trends, many still have a pension benefit from one or more employers during their working career. Like the decision about Social Security, the decision on the pension benefit amount is irrevocable and involves unknown factors, such as longevity. Let's use an example to see the relationship of the amount of the monthly benefits to the potential length of time those benefits are received.

Ken is married and has worked for twenty-two years at a manufacturer of car parts. Three months prior to his retirement, he met with an employee from the human resources department at his company to review his pension options. She presented Ken with the following:

1. Monthly pension benefits at age sixty-five for
   Ken's life only $ 1,546

2. 50-percent surviving spouse option:
   Monthly pension benefits at age sixty-five for
   Ken's life $ 1,306
   50 percent of monthly benefit over surviving
   spouse's life $ 653

3. 100-percent contingent annuitant option
   (a beneficiary named by Ken, such as spouse or
   other, receives the same monthly benefit as Ken) $ 1,219

4. Lump-sum option (pension received at once,
   not monthly) $125,000

The pension benefit calculation is specific to Ken and will differ for every individual at Ken's company. This is because the monthly amounts depend on Ken's age, his spouse's age, his salary, and his years of service. Some companies do not offer a lump-sum option. But our approach to analyzing Ken's options can still apply to you.

Which option should Ken choose? Like the answer to most complex questions, it depends. You can see the trade-off in the monthly amounts on the previous page: more monthly income immediately or a lower monthly income for potentially more years.

If Ken wants the highest amount of current income, then he would choose option 1 for his life only. To obtain this higher monthly benefit, he is taking a risk. If he dies after only a few years, then his surviving spouse (or heirs) receives nothing.

Generally, we would not recommend this "one life only" option if you are married. We feel that this does not help provide for your surviving spouse. Our biblical basis is found in 1 Timothy 5:8, *"But if anyone does not provide for his own, and especially for those of his household, he has denied the faith, and is worse than an unbeliever."*

Unfortunately, we have seen actual cases where a family had debt or a costly lifestyle. This situation motivated them to choose the higher monthly benefit. Then, the pension participant died sooner than expected, leaving his surviving spouse without a monthly income benefit. (As a note, most pension plans require the spouse to sign an acknowledgment before a married pension participant chooses an option without surviving spouse benefits.)

If Ken wanted his spouse to receive the same monthly benefit as he received during his life (instead of a 50-percent reduction), then he would select the 100-percent contingent annuitant option. This monthly benefit is lower than the 50-percent surviving spouse option ($1,219 vs. $1,306). Ken may consider this 100-percent option if he has other sources of earnings now, such as part-time work. If he were to die, then his part-time income would also disappear. So his wife may need the same pension income after his death to make ends meet. Ken may also consider this option if he estimates his wife is likely to live longer than average.

Some pension plans offer the lump-sum option. The lump-sum option offers an enticing temptation. When offered, this option is often the most popular but also the least valuable to the employee. The lump-sum option is usually structured to be worth less than the monthly benefits, but as many as 90 percent of departing employees choose the lump sum without realizing it has far less value.[4]

Perhaps the lump sum is so appealing because it is more money than most of us would see all at once. Given the choice of $125,000 or $1,219 a month, most would choose the $125,000. But the $1,219 per month over two lives could easily result in total payments exceeding $300,000 or $400,000. The lack of information provided by employers to compare adequately the lump-sum option to the monthly benefit option has become a problem. At the time of this writing, both the Treasury Department and the U.S. Senate are proposing regulations forcing employers to provide more "apples to apples" comparisons for employees.[5]

An advantage of the lump-sum option is that Ken would have control over the money immediately. Of course, this could be a disadvantage to Ken and his family if he is prone to spend foolishly or to invest unwisely. Another advantage is the elimination of the "dying too soon" risk. Even if Ken and his spouse died prematurely, his estate would still have the benefit of the pension lump sum. Under some monthly payment options, the heirs would receive no benefit.

When would the lump-sum option make sense? If Ken's surviving spouse has a substantial pension available from her own career or if both Ken and his wife experience poor health.

We have presented throughout this book the increased longevity trends and the fear of outliving your income. With this in mind, we generally believe that if you have a pension, then you are better served by choosing pension options that pay a lifetime benefit for both you and at least 50 percent for your surviving spouse. Individual circumstances will vary and may warrant another option, which is why we included chapter 3 about decision making.

INCOME FROM INVESTMENTS

Interest and dividend income, or even the gradual use of investment principal, will likely compose a portion of your income as you grow older. The aim of retirement planning during earlier stages of life is to accumulate assets for when you slow down.

Perhaps you have accumulated assets in Individual Retirement Accounts (IRAs), company 401(k) accounts, or brokerage accounts. If so, then you have wisely taken some steps to plan for the "winter." As Proverbs 6:6–8 says, *"Go to the ant, O sluggard, observe her ways and be wise, which, having no chief, officer or ruler, prepares her food in the summer and gathers her provision in the harvest."*

At some point, you will begin to withdraw money from these investments to live on when other income sources fade or to fund a lasting legacy (see chapter 10). This transition from the accumulation phase to the distribution phase is sometimes a hard one to make psychologically. Why are withdrawals difficult? We can think of a few reasons:

1. *An admission of getting older.* You are no longer in your prime earning years, socking away money for retirement. You are on the other side of the hill now and need withdrawals.

2. *No more hoarding allowed.* As money accumulates inside of an IRA or 401(k), you can sometimes be prone to pride at the amounts amassed. If you are not careful, then the game to see how much you can save can border on hoarding. But when withdrawals begin, the balances begin to drop and the game is not so much fun anymore.

3. *Uncertainty of having enough to last.* Beginning withdrawals reminds you of the uncertainty of knowing how much to withdraw, how long you will live, and whether you will have enough to last.

But remember the ant. The ant knows why it is saving. The ant is not upset that it needs in the winter what it stored in the harvest of late summer.

Much is written about the importance of saving, using IRAs and 401(k) accounts, but little is said about the withdrawal phase. Let's briefly review the tax rules and limits with these tax-deferred savings. Tax-deferred savings include 401(k) accounts, traditional IRAs, Keogh and profit sharing plans, fixed annuities, and variable annuities. Remember that *tax deferred* means you have postponed the income tax through the years. You have never paid income tax on the increase each year while assets were accumulating.

Because you received the tax benefits of delaying taxation on the earnings of tax-deferred savings, Congress and the IRS have some strings attached. First, you generally cannot withdraw money from these plans before age fifty-nine and a half without a penalty. Talk to your accountant about certain exceptions for withdrawals before fifty-nine and a half.

Second, you must generally begin at least a minimum amount of withdrawals at age seventy and a half or face penalties. In other words, you cannot defer the income tax indefinitely. An exception applies to the general rule of seventy and a half if you have not yet retired. You can postpone the minimum required distributions until April 1 of the year following the year you retire.

The minimum amount to withdraw at age seventy and a half is based on IRS mortality tables. If you have $100,000 in an IRA at age seventy and a half, then your minimum required distribution would be $3,650 per year ($100,000 divided by the IRS table factor of 27.4).

You would always have the freedom to withdraw all or a portion of your tax-deferred savings without penalty at any time after age fifty-nine and a half. You also can withdraw more than your required minimum distribution after age seventy and a half.

Withdrawals from tax-deferred savings are a balancing act. On the one hand, wise financial planning usually means you defer income taxes for as long as possible. But, on the other hand, leaving a significant 401(k) or traditional IRA to your children or grandchildren will result in more taxes paid if they are in a higher tax bracket than you.

Nonspousal beneficiaries, such as an adult child, must pay income taxes on the tax-deferred savings. Why? Because the original owner of the traditional IRA had never paid income taxes on it.

Let's say that Marilyn, a sixty-eight-year-old widow, received a traditional IRA worth $250,000 from her deceased husband. Marilyn has few sources of income and is in the lowest income tax bracket of 10 percent. Marilyn passes away and leaves the IRA to her children, Jacob, an attorney, and Sharon, an advertising executive. Jacob and Sharon are both in the higher 30 percent income tax bracket. They must begin receiving income from the inherited traditional IRA either all at once or over their lifetimes. Then they must pay income tax at their tax rates. The family would have paid less tax overall if Marilyn, the widowed mother, had begun receiving more distributions and paying income tax at her lower rates than her children's higher rates.

Many of you reading this may have parents in similar situations. If so, encourage them to talk with their accountant and advisers to begin traditional IRA or 401(k) distributions. If those parents do not need the money immediately, then they can continue to invest it outside of a traditional IRA or give it away.

What bucket of investment money do you spend first? Remember that you have already paid at least part of the tax on taxable investment accounts [that is, non-IRAs, non-401(k)s]. Therefore this money goes further than tax-deferred savings where you must pay income tax. Let's say that you are adding a garage to your house and need $10,000. If you withdraw money from a traditional IRA, then you really have to withdraw almost $15,000 to end up with a net amount of $10,000 if you are in the 28 percent tax bracket for federal and 5 percent for state. But if you use money from a taxable account, such as a mutual fund or CD, then you use up less principal by withdrawing only what you need.

A word about an IRA named Roth. Beginning in 1998, Roth IRAs, named after Senator Roth from Delaware who proposed the legislation, became available to qualifying earners. The main benefit of the Roth IRA is that the earnings are tax free, not tax deferred. Contributions are not tax deductible, but all future growth of the investments within a Roth IRA is tax free.

Another benefit of the Roth IRA is that no minimum distributions are required at age seventy and a half. Assets can grow inside a Roth IRA for the owner's lifetime and then can be passed on to adult children or grandchildren and continue growing with no tax ever to be paid. Roth IRAs are much more useful as estate planning vehicles than traditional IRAs or 401(k)s.

To qualify, you must have earned income, that is earnings from work—one more reason to have a part-time job. You also must have an adjusted gross income less than $150,000 for married filing jointly or $95,000 for a single filer.

We recommend using a Roth IRA whenever possible to shield future income from taxes.

How much can I withdraw from investments and not run out of money? As is often our answer, it depends. Choosing an appropriate withdrawal rate is an important analysis but yet another example of an Impossible Decision. A key factor is how much your investments will continue earning. You'll have to assume a rate of return for now. Then, look at the table below to see how many years your investments will last. The first column going down is the percentage withdrawal rate you make, while the top row going across is the rate of return the remaining investments earn. The number in the block where the withdrawal rate and rate of return intersect is how many years your investment pool will remain.

Rate of Return on Investments										
With-drawal Rate	1%	2%	3%	4%	5%	6%	7%	8%	9%	10%
12%	7	8	8	8	8	9	9	10	10	11
11	8	8	9	9	9	10	10	11	12	13
10	9	9	10	10	10	11	12	13	14	15
9	10	10	11	11	12	13	14	15	16	18
8	11	11	12	13	14	15	16	18	20	24
7	12	13	14	15	**16**	18	20	22	27	36
6	14	15	16	18	19	22	25	31	44	>50
5	17	18	20	22	24	29	36	>50	>50	>50
4	20	22	25	28	33	42	>50	>50	>50	>50
3	25	28	33	39	>50	>50	>50	>50	>50	>50
2	35	40	50	>50	>50	>50	>50	>50	>50	>50
1	>50	>50	>50	>50	>50	>50	>50	>50	>50	>50

Source: Kiplinger's Personal Finance Magazine, October 1998

Let's walk through an example and use the table.

1. Figure how much income from your investments you will need each year. Simply add up your total living expenses (including taxes from any tax-deferred withdrawals) and subtract the regular income you have from other sources.

    Example: Ed and Jill have $35,000 of expenses. Their combined Social Security, pension, and part-time work is $25,000.

2. Add up your total investment portfolio (both tax-deferred savings and other assets).

> Example: Ed and Jill have a total of $150,000 consisting of $100,000 in IRAs, $25,000 in mutual funds outside of IRAs, and $25,000 in a certificate of deposit.

3. Divide the amount needed from your investments by the total investments. Multiply by 100 to obtain the withdrawal percentage rate.

> Example: Ed and Jill have a withdrawal rate of 6.67 percent, which is closest to 7 percent ($10,000 divided by $150,000 x 100).

4. Estimate your annual rate of return on your investments.

> Example: Ed and Jill estimate an annual return of 5 percent based on their investment allocation and past results.

5. Find the withdrawal rate and annual rate of return on the table.

> Example: Ed and Jill can expect their investment principle to last sixteen years.

Please note that the table assumes your initial withdrawal rate (7 percent in the case of Ed and Jill) will increase annually to keep up with an estimated 3 percent inflation. This is why using the table above you can still run out of money even if you use the same withdrawal rate and rate of return. That's the effect of inflation.

Speaking of inflation. Even though inflation has been fairly tame in the U.S. during recent years, it remains your primary enemy during retirement. A car costing $20,000 today will cost more than $43,000 in twenty years at an inflation rate of 4 percent. At an inflation rate of 3 percent per year, prices will double every twenty-four years.

Let's consider this for a moment. If you retire at age sixty, your cost of living will double when you reach eighty-four. Therefore, try to structure your sources of income to increase along with inflation.

Convert assets to an income stream with annuities. Annuities are confusing because there are two types of annuities and two phases of annuities. The two types are *fixed*, which offer a fixed rate of interest (similar to a CD), and *variable*, which offer a variable return depending on how the investments perform (similar to a mutual fund). Insurance companies, with their knowledge of mortality tables, issue annuities. Charitable institutions also provide annuities in coordinating planned giving.

Both types of annuities have two phases: the accumulation phase (deferred) and the distribution phase (immediate). Most attention is placed on the accumulation phase, the time period that you contribute and try to build the total assets within the annuity. You may purchase an annuity and begin at either point: the accumulation phase or the distribution phase. We will focus, however, on the distribution side because that is what yields income.

An immediate annuity is simply a contract guaranteeing a lifetime income. Let's assume that Phil, age sixty-five, purchases an immediate fixed annuity for $50,000. He is beginning the distribution phase immediately. Then, he will receive $353 per month for the rest of his life.[6]

What if Phil dies three years later after beginning the immediate annuity? Well, that's it. The insurance company wins. What if Phil lives to be ninety-eight years old? He gets a payment every single month of his life; in other words, he wins and the insurance company loses. Phil could select several options, such as a minimum twenty-year payout, but his monthly income would drop from $353 to $313 per month. The minimum, or "certain," payout period is the guaranteed period of time that Phil or his beneficiaries would receive a monthly payment.

In essence, immediate annuities are "longevity insurance." Young fathers buy life insurance in case they die too soon. You would buy an immediate annuity in case you were to live too long.

If Phil waited until age seventy, the same $50,000 would buy an annuity paying him $398 per month. It pays more because Phil will likely not live as long (or receive as many payments) as he did at sixty-five.

Immediate annuities are an excellent way to ensure that you will have income to last. This is particularly true if you do not have a pension from past employers; you can create your own pension with an immediate annuity.

To obtain all the good benefits of an immediate annuity, you have to put up with a downside: giving up irrevocably some of your savings or capital. If a sixty-five-year-old man needed an income of $700 per month, he would have to pay approximately $100,000 for an immediate annuity.

Here are a few tips on buying immediate annuities.

- Buy from high-rated, financially strong insurers.
- Don't use all of your savings to buy an annuity.
- Buy as late as you can.
- Buy for only as much income as you need (you can always buy another one later if needed).
- Spend no more than $100,000 per insurer.
- Obtain a joint-and-survivor annuity if married to pay income for as long as one of you lives.

In addition to our discussion on Social Security, work pensions, and annuities in this chapter, we would like to examine investment principles further in the next chapter. Your investments comprise assets that can provide an income stream to last and possibly a significant amount to leave as a legacy.

ASK RON

Q. How do you plan to decide about Social Security for yourself?

A. At the writing of this book, I am sixty-two. My plans are to delay Social Security until full retirement age. As I mentioned in chapter 4, my "rehirement" plans are to continue earning some income even though I will have different vocational pursuits. It looks to me like beginning my Social Security benefits at full retirement age is the best mathematical option due to my earning more than the Social Security limits. I do not think that waiting until age seventy is a wise choice because I would permanently lose the benefits during the years from sixty-five to seventy.

ASK LARRY

Q. How did you decide about whether to take Social Security at sixty-two or later?

A. For me, that was an easy issue. I am waiting until the full retirement age of sixty-five. Even though I had been diagnosed with cancer well before age sixty-two, I wanted to keep working. Many people might say that having cancer would be a reason to begin benefits as soon as possible. But as I have already mentioned, I aim to continue working at what God has called me to do until I can no longer be effective for Him. I did not think it would be wise to begin receiving Social Security benefits and have them be reduced by what I was earning from my working and writing.

ASK RON

Q. What is a sustainable withdrawal rate that you assume from IRAs and 401(k)s?

A. I don't have a working rule-of-thumb rate for withdrawals. It depends on the investment rate of return. If you are invested in the stock market, then you would be wise and conservative to assume an 8 percent growth rate. If you have a portfolio that is 60 percent bonds and 40 percent stocks, then assume a lower rate of return, say 5 percent. Then you can compare potential withdrawal rates in the table presented in this chapter against these rates of return.

ASK LARRY

Q. What percentage of income should a person secure?

A. In my situation, because of my cancer, I have tried to secure 100 percent of my income. This means that I reduced my stock market investments and moved to fixed income (bonds, CDs, etc.) to provide my wife with enough income to live on.

The answer to this question depends upon, to some extent, the security you have of other income. You may have a business or rental houses that will provide ongoing income for some time. For a salaried person, I think you probably need to try to secure 70 to 90 percent of your income. I find that expenses do not go down as much as you may think when you change your vocation or when you retire. They go down in some areas, but they go up in others.

ASK YOURSELF

- Reflecting upon my family history of longevity, my current health, and my lifestyle, would I expect to have less than expected longevity, average longevity, or more than expected longevity?
- What sources of income will I have available to me during my later years?
- Have I received a pension estimate from my employer and a Social Security statement from the Social Security Administration so I can know how much additional income to plan on providing through other sources?
- How can I anticipate and prepare for the various employment opportunities that will be available to me?
- What would I do if any of the sources of retirement income that I anticipate were to have less than expected results?

CHAPTER 6

Invest to Last

— OR —

"Want to Safely Double Your Money? Fold It Over Once and Put It in Your Pocket"

Only a fool tests the depth of the water with both feet.
AFRICAN PROVERB

There are two times in a man's life when he should not speculate:
when he can't afford it, and when he can.
MARK TWAIN

She considers a field and buys it;
From her earnings she plants a vineyard.
PROVERBS 31:16

Divide your portion to seven, or even to eight, for you do not know
what misfortune may occur on the earth.
ECCLESIASTES 11:2

A Chinese parable tells a perceptive story about a rural family long ago. The family had a horse that helped to plow the land and raise their food.

One day the horse ran away while the farmer's son was plowing in the field. Neighbors came and said to the old man and the boy, "We heard about your bad luck. It is so bad."

"How do you know it is bad?" answered the farmer. "It is not over yet."

Sure enough, in a few days the horse came back leading a herd of wild horses. "We heard about your good luck and came to congratulate you," said the neighbors.

"How do you know it is good luck?" answered the farmer. "It is not over yet."

A few days later while the boy was trying to train one of the horses, it threw him and broke his leg. "Oh," said the neighbors, "we heard about your bad luck and came to sympathize."

Again the old man replied, "How do you know it is bad? It is not over yet."

The parable ends by saying that a great war came, and all the able-bodied young men were taken off to fight. But the boy with the broken leg stayed at home and cared for his aging father for the rest of his days.

We can't even estimate how many times we have heard people tell us how upset they are with the decline in their investments. They open their statements in the mail and then open their medication.

We understand. No one enjoys seeing the value of their investments decline. But we often respond, "When will you need the money from this investment?" Many times the answer is, "Not for another ten years or so." Then, as the Chinese farmer said, "It is not over yet."

During the inevitable periods of decline, remember that *market loss* is different from *market fluctuation*. Market loss is when you actually sell and realize a loss. It is what Enron employees experienced. Their company filed bankruptcy, and their company stock in 401(k)s lost all its value.

Market fluctuation is the regular change in value as measured from one point in time to another certain point in time. If you have not sold yet, then you are at the "not over yet" point. All of your assets are subject to market fluctuation; you just don't see it or get a quarterly statement.

What if you received a statement at the end of the fourth quarter for your house? Housing prices, like stock prices, are determined by supply and demand. Let's say that a local factory announced a layoff on December 1. Any realtor will likely tell you that late December is a slow time in the housing market. So the arbitrary date to send a statement on December 31 may reflect a decline in value from the previous quarter. Does that mean you have experienced a market loss? No, only a market fluctuation. If you don't sell your house on the statement date, then you have not experienced a market loss. The same is true with your investments.

Instead of one chapter, we could write an entire book on investments. In fact, we have both done just that. Larry has written *Investing for the Future*, and Ron has written *Storm Shelter.* To keep this book a size that can still be portable, we will focus on the biblical reasoning for investing and key principles for those age fifty and over aiming to make their investments last.

INVESTING: THE WHAT, WHO, AND WHEN

Investing is simply taking a reasonable risk to reap a future reward. It is the management of money to generate a potential profit. The first investment can be found in Genesis 3:23. Adam was cast out of the garden and told to cultivate the soil for his food. To do so, he had to risk seeds that could have been eaten; thus, he became an investor.

Every farmer understands investing—taking a risk to reap a reward. Each year he is faced with a choice of eating all the seeds, selling all the seeds, or retaining some to replant. It would be a shortsighted farmer who would either eat or sell his entire harvest. A wise farmer not only holds back some seed for replanting, but he also sorts out some of the best seed to ensure a greater harvest. By doing so he exercises self-discipline to achieve greater prosperity.

Contrary to what many people believe, God is not against prosperity. The Scriptures give evidence that prosperity is one of God's blessings to those who love and obey Him (2 Chronicles 16:9; Psalm 37:4; Proverbs 8:21). But we must guard ourselves against greed, covetousness, and pride. Investing for selfish reasons breeds these attitudes.

Sometimes Christians are confused about investing. Some dedicate their entire lives to investing, thinking that somehow they can buffer themselves from all the world's ills simply by having enough assets. Doug is that way. He is constantly thinking about how much he has, how much it goes up or down, and how major world events affect his portfolio.

Doug checks his investment account first thing each morning on the Internet before reading his Bible. He gets more upset about a down day on the Dow than he does about the spiritual condition of his neighbor. He regularly repeats to himself that he is doing it for his family and is trying to be a good steward. But he daydreams during sermons about his assets and financial plans.

Sitting on the pew in front of Doug at church is Millie. She remembers her father losing money in the stock market during the Great Depression. Combining memories of her father's disdain of financial markets with a mixture of sermons denouncing worldliness, she believes investing is practically sinful. Millie staunchly believes that investing is a secular enterprise, and good Christians should have nothing to do with it. She puts her money in the bank where it is insured and hides cash in secret places in her house.

Both of these views are unbalanced. God's Word supports investing, but it's always to satisfy future needs: supplementing income in old age, providing for and educating children, and storing up some wealth for future needs within the body of Christ. These and many other activities are perfectly legitimate according to God's Word. Investing in and of itself is not sinful, but the attitude behind investing may be sinful.

WORLDLY MOTIVES FOR INVESTING

Unfortunately, the worldly motives for investing represent the most common motives of investors, both Christian and non-Christian, because Satan has so thoroughly dominated our attitudes about money.

Greed. The continual desire to have more and demand only the best available. *"But those who want to get rich fall into temptation and a snare and many foolish and harmful desires which plunge men into ruin and destruction"* (1 Timothy 6:9).

Pride. The desire to receive admiration and respect because of material achievements. *"Instruct those who are rich in this present world not to be conceited or to fix their hope on the uncertainty of riches, but on God, who richly supplies us with all things to enjoy"* (1 Timothy 6:17).

Ignorance. Following the counsel of other misguided people because of a lack of discernment. *"Leave the presence of a fool, or you will not discern words of knowledge"* (Proverbs 14:7).

Envy. The desire to achieve based on observation of other people's success. *"For I was envious of the arrogant, as I saw the prosperity of the wicked"* (Psalm 73:3).

The bottom line is simply that worldly motives reflect worldly values. The results of worldly values are anxiety, frustration, and eventually a deadening of spiritual values. Thus, as our Lord says, *"No servant can serve two masters; for either he will hate the one and love the other, or else he will be devoted to one and despise the other. You cannot serve God and wealth*" (Luke 16:13).

BIBLICAL MOTIVES FOR INVESTING

The scriptural justification for investing is to multiply current assets to meet future *needs* for you or others. Note our emphasis on *needs*, not on expanding wants and desires as your income increases. Biblical motives for investing include the following.

To further God's work. Some Christians have received a gift of giving (Romans 12:8). To them the multiplication of material worth is an extension of their basic ministry within the body of Christ. Even to those who do not have a gift of giving, investments are a way to preserve and multiply a surplus that has been provided for a later time. In Acts 4:34, the believers sold their assets and surrendered the proceeds to meet the needs of other believers. God blesses some with an earlier surplus to be used at a later date.

Family responsibility. We are admonished to provide for those within our own households (1 Timothy 5:8). In the Old Testament that provision was never limited to the life span of a father. It extended to providing for the family even after the father's death.

Future needs. If parents believe God wants their children to go to college, is it more spiritual to expect the government to educate them than to store for the eventual need? The parable of the ant in Proverbs 6:6 says to *"observe her ways and be wise."* One of her ways is to plan ahead by storing. In an inflationary economy, even storing requires investing to maintain purchasing power.

WHAT TO INVEST

If you read no more of this chapter, read this truth: Only invest your surplus. Sounds simple, but this principle can protect you from economic ruin. You invest your excess after paying regular expenses and consumer debt. In our information-saturated society of instant Internet financial quotes and cable financial networks, people sometimes think they are smarter, more sophisticated, or beyond simple truths that sound as if they came from Grandma.

When certain investments are popular, many borrow to invest. Actions such as buying on margin, taking out a home equity loan to invest in the market, and investing instead of paying credit-card debt all violate this truth.

As we pointed out in chapter 2 in the sequential steps of investing, invest only upon reaching steps 5 and 6. These steps are *after* you have paid off high-interest debt and have adequate savings. Don't take risks with money that you need to live on or to pay debt with.

How to Handle a Surplus

A Christian businessman asked a pertinent question: "I have a surplus of money each year. What am I to do with it: give it away, invest it, put it into a retirement plan, or what?" On the surface the Bible would seem to be confusing on this issue. One proverb says a wise man has a surplus in his home while a fool has bare cupboards. However, another says that a poor man has God's blessings and a rich man is a fool. Even the parables of Christ appear somewhat confusing. In one parable He rebuked a rich fool who built larger barns to store his surplus, and in another He rebuked the man who failed to invest a large surplus wisely.

God's Word is always right and is never in conflict. In the various passages mentioned above, God is dealing with heart attitudes or motives. In each situation the motives must be analyzed. For one person a surplus of money represents a trust from God that can be used for current and future needs. For another it represents a trap of Satan to lead him out of God's path.

The certainty is that Scripture warns that there is a greater danger in having a surplus than in having a need. *"And Jesus looked at him and said, 'How hard it is for those who are wealthy to enter the kingdom of God! For it is easier for a camel to go through the eye of a needle than for a rich man to enter the kingdom of God'"* (Luke 18:24–25).

For those Christians with a surplus of money provided by God to meet future needs, good stewardship of that surplus requires that some or all of it be invested. God has provided a great surplus to many Christians today.

Many Christians firmly believe that there is no scriptural justification for investing while others have a lack. That simply is not true. The justification for anyone's investing is that he has given cheerfully what God has led him to give. He has met the reasonable needs of his family, and he still has a surplus.

An important prerequisite for investing is attitude. Why are you investing, and how will the surplus be used? If a Christian wants God to entrust greater riches to him, he must be found faithful in the smaller amount first. *"He who is faithful in a very little thing is faithful also in much; and he who is unrighteous in a very little thing is unrighteous also in much. Therefore if you have not been faithful in the use of unrighteous wealth, who will entrust the true riches to you?"* (Luke 16:10–11).

How Much to Invest

To protect against the infectious diseases of greed and pride, the best weapon is a specific plan for returning the excess to God's Kingdom. This means determining what is the maximum you need to live on, or defining your "finish line." We find that once a commitment has been made to a disciplined lifestyle, regardless of the available income, the dangers of greed and self-indulgence are significantly reduced.

Once a Christian has accepted the purpose of investing to serve God better, the crucial decision is how much to invest. Obviously, there is no absolute answer. It is an individual decision made by each Christian after much prayer. With earnest prayer the decision is difficult; without it, impossible. However, some initial choices will greatly simplify your decision about how much to invest.

1. Give to God's work. Give until you know that all the needs God has placed on your heart are satisfied. This doesn't mean there will be no more needs in the world. There will always be needs, but God doesn't place every need on every heart. Giving, like spiritual discernment, is a matter of growth and practice. One suggestion is, "When in doubt, give." It is better to be wrong and give too much than to ignore God's direction and give too little. Being too sensitive never dampens the Spirit; only a callused heart that ignores His nudging dampens the Spirit. *"Therefore openly before the churches, show them the proof of your love and of our reason for boasting about you"* (2 Corinthians 8:24).

2. Control personal spending. Settle on a lifestyle level that is God's plan for you. Too much spending by a family can rob surplus funds as surely as bad investments. Each Christian family must decide on the level God has planned for them and stick to it in spite of available surpluses. Remember that balance is essential. Too much spending breeds indulgence; too little is self-punishment. *"And whatever we ask we receive from Him, because we keep His commandments and do the things that are pleasing in His sight"* (1 John 3:22).

3. Develop a written plan. Have a plan for the use of your potential surpluses. One interesting characteristic about humans is that we can rationalize nearly anything, including reinvesting God's portion or saving it for Him. Therefore, it is important to settle on a plan for distributing the profits from investments before they arrive. Decide what portion is to be reinvested. Clearly, a danger is to reinvest continually the profits and rationalize it because of tax planning, lack of discernible needs, or a fear of the future. A written plan holds you accountable. *"Because of the proof given by this ministry they will glorify God for your obedience to your confession of the gospel of Christ and for the liberality of your contribution to them and to all"* (2 Corinthians 9:13).

INVESTING: THE HOW

Just as the sages of real-estate investing emphasize location, we would say that building an investment portfolio to last depends on three factors: diversification, diversification, diversification. Solomon, in his wisdom, offers an excellent investment strategy in Ecclesiastes 11:2, *"Divide your portion to seven, or even eight, for you do not know what misfortune may occur on the earth."*

The sustained rise in the stock market during the 1980s and 1990s provided significant increases in the value of 401(k)s, IRAs, and personal investments. However, many realized too late that they were not properly diversified. As Warren Buffet stated, "A rising tide does lift all boats, but when the tide goes out, you see who has been swimming naked."

DIVERSIFICATION: A STRATEGY THAT WORKS

Diversification is spreading your money among different types of investments. By doing so, you diminish your overall risk.

A retired couple wanted to start a small business in the mountains of North Carolina. They were leaning toward opening a cozy gourmet coffee shop when a friend intervened. The coffee shop, he pointed out, would be a welcome retreat from the brisk autumn breezes and winter snows, but sales were apt to be sluggish during the hot summer months.

Rethinking their plan, the couple decided to open a coffee and ice cream shop. If coffee sales lagged in the heat, the promise of ice cream would lure the summertime crowds. Similarly, a hot cup of coffee would keep the winter customers coming even if ice cream sales melted. By diversifying their offerings, the couple had hit upon a plan that would reduce their overall risk while enhancing their total return.

DIVERSIFICATION SEQUENCE

A portfolio is a group of individual investments. When I (Ron) help a client of our firm structure his or her investment portfolio, we follow a sequential strategy that includes diversification among several categories (see figure below).

By moving from one category to the next, this approach gives an investor the ability to diversify within diversification, thereby strengthening the total portfolio.

The Diversification Hierarchy

Diversification by Asset Class and Category

Diversification by asset class is the most widely practiced form of diversification. It involves combining different assets—such as stocks, bonds, international investments, and real estate—into a single portfolio. Because these various assets have different risk and return characteristics, they rise and fall in value independent of one another. By combining two or more asset classes, you can reduce the volatility, or risk, in the portfolio.

Asset categories are a subgroup of asset classes. A smart diversification strategy includes investments in different categories within each asset class. This chart highlights asset classes and categories and offers some common examples in each category.

Asset Class	Category	Example
Stocks	Large Company	Dow Jones Industrials, Blue Chips
	Small Company	NASDAQ, Speculative
International	Developed Markets	Germany, Great Britain, Japan
	Emerging and Developing Markets	Mexico, Chile, Singapore, Thailand
Bonds	Government	Treasury Notes/Bills, Series EE
	Corporate	Bonds, Debentures
	Municipal	Airport Authority, County Revenue and Sales Tax
	Speculative	Junk, International, Mortgage
	Mortgage Pools	GNMA, FNMA
Real Estate	Income-Producing	Apartment Complex, Building Space
	Non-Income-Producing	Raw Land
	Stocks	REITs
Precious Metals	Gold and Silver	Kruggerands, Coins, Bars
Cash	Cash/Cash Equivalent Bank	Money-Market Fund, CDs
(Note: When you begin to build your own portfolio, the cash asset class will not be included in your asset allocation. Your cash positions must be maintained in liquid investments to cover living expenses and any emergencies that might arise.)		

Diversification by Investment Style

An investment style is the strategy used for buying and selling investments. A mutual fund manager may employ a *value style*. *Value* investors look for stocks or bonds that are selling below what people generally

consider to be a reasonable value. The assumption is that an underval-
ued stock price represents a good deal. Other mutual fund managers
operate with a *growth style*. *Growth* investors evaluate stocks based on
a company's quarterly earnings report and its expectations of future
earnings.

Different investment styles become popular at different times similar
to different fashions coming in vogue from time to time. During the bull
market of the late 1990s, the growth style was popular as growth stocks
led the market for several years. Then, when the market endured losses
in the early 2000s, the value style performed much better than growth.

The best-diversified portfolios incorporate a combination of two or
more investment styles at all times. Try to avoid chasing the most recent
popular style. By the time you get on board, a style that was effective at
one time may be less effective when you invest in it. Doing what the
crowd does may work well in picking a good restaurant but not in picking good investments.

This comparison of styles applies only to stocks and bonds. In reality, there are as many styles of investing as there are investment managers.
Each investment manager may have a basic style but change it or fine-
tune it to meet his or her own personality, experience, and objectives.
There are also different styles within different asset classes. The point is
that different styles perform differently in various scenarios; therefore,
diversification by manager style within asset classes is a further protection
against risk of loss. Investing purely in one style, even if other diversification methods are used, will still expose you to unnecessary risks.

Diversification by Manager

Within each asset class and investment style an investor can diversify by
relying on several different managers (or funds with different managers).
As Proverbs 11:14 says, victory comes with an *"abundance of counselors."*

Given the varying specializations and knowledge of different investment managers, it makes sense to take advantage of the combined expertise of a group of professionals. Also, because each manager has his own biases and blind spots, using several managers (or funds) reduces the risk of a portfolio's being severely damaged by the poor performance of any one individual.

Diversification over Time

Diversification over time works through two strategies, one used for fixed-income investments and one that works with growth-oriented investments.

Fixed-income investments, such as bonds, benefit from diversification over time when maturity dates are staggered. A bond's maturity date is the date that the bond (or the loan an investor made to the bond issuer) comes due. Until that time the issuer makes regular payments on the loan, which reflect the interest rate at which the bond was purchased.

Short-term bonds mature between one and five years. Intermediate-term bonds come due in five to ten years. And long-term bonds mature after ten to thirty years.

Because bonds make payments according to the interest rate at the time the bond was purchased, it is possible to have a long-term bond that offers a much greater return than that which is currently available. A portfolio that includes bonds with staggered maturity dates takes advantage of the fact that as interest rates increase, assets will be available to purchase new bonds; and, as interest rates decrease, existing bonds will outperform their newer counterparts.

Dollar cost averaging is the second time-diversification strategy. This technique, used to purchase stocks and mutual funds, offers an excellent way to invest on a periodic basis. Monthly savings or annual

IRA contributions can be used to dollar cost average. Because the value of stocks and mutual funds fluctuates over time, it is impossible to pinpoint the best time to make a purchase. By staggering your purchases, you can lower your risk of entering the market at a high point. Instead, you pursue the average price.

The idea behind dollar cost averaging is to invest a regular amount of money in a particular stock or mutual fund on a regular basis. This strategy allows you to ignore market swings and, over time, achieve an average rate of return. If you participate in a retirement plan through payroll deductions, you are already dollar cost averaging.

Diversification by Geography

Real estate represents an investment that can benefit from geographical diversification. We have known people, such as those investing in the Texas oil boom of the 1970s and early 1980s, who experienced financial ruin because their real-estate investments were not diversified by geography. Real-estate investment trusts (REITs) pool assets in order to buy land or real-estate projects in several cities or states.

International investments comprise another asset class that could be geographically diversified. Emerging markets, such as those in Mexico and Singapore, may offer excellent growth potential. Developed countries, such as Japan and Great Britain, offer market opportunities that are relatively insulated from some of the systematic risk that drives the U.S. markets.

(Note: International investments are best pursued through a professional manager or mutual fund. Also, because of the volatile nature of some emerging markets, only investors with an aggressive risk tolerance should consider these funds.)

Moving to Application

We realize that we have presented quite a bit of information. Let's try to apply these concepts to your personal situation.

We recommend that you sit down with a qualified investment adviser you can trust and design a plan that will meet your God-directed goals. If you use the services of an adviser, then much of the adviser's job is helping to diversify your portfolio. Therefore, you may not wish to work through the next few pages. Or, even though you use an adviser, you may wish to review your portfolio in these next few pages and discuss the results with your adviser. Certainly, if you handle your investment portfolio yourself, then you need to determine how diversified you are.

Step 1: Determine your risk tolerance

How you should invest your money depends on how much risk you're comfortable taking. Financial advisers call this your risk tolerance. When you read about, or if an adviser asks you about your risk tolerance, you may give a little shrug of the shoulders and say you don't know.

To help identify your risk tolerance, we have nine simple questions. The following questions may help you determine your tolerance for risk and the best types of investments for you. There are no absolute right or wrong answers. Mark your response to each question, write the point value on the line, and then add up the score.

Investor Profile Questionnaire

Would you take out money from your account before retirement to pay for a large, unexpected expense?	☐ Yes . . . . 0 points ☐ No. . . . . 10 points ☐ Maybe . . . . 4 points <div align="right">Points_____</div>

Have you ever invested in individual stocks or stock accounts?	☐ Yes, and I was uncomfortable with the risk . . 0 points
	☐ Yes, and I was comfortable with the risk . . . 13 points
	☐ No, but I would feel uncomfortable with the
	   risk if I did . . . . 3 points
	☐ No, but I would feel comfortable with the risk
	   if I did . . . . 8 points
	<div align="right">Points_____</div>

Assume you have $1,000 invested in an account, and its value dropped to $850 after six months. What would you do?	☐ I'd move all of the money to a more
	   conservative account. . . . . .0 points
	☐ I wouldn't make any changes. . . . . 13 points
	☐ I'd transfer some money to a more
	   conservative account. . . . . .4 points
	☐ I'd put more money into that account . . . . . 16 points
	<div align="right">Points_____</div>

If your retirement plan offered two or more stock accounts, which best describes the one you would choose?	☐ An account that invests in big established
	   companies that have a solid track record of
	   earnings and dividends. These are among
	   the least risky stock accounts . . . . 6 points
	☐ An account that invests in small growing companies
	   that pay few dividends but have significant
	   long-term growth potential. These are among
	   the most risky stock accounts . . . . 14 points
	☐ More than one account, dividing my money
	   between large and small company stock
	   accounts . . . . 10 points
	☐ No stock accounts—the market is too risky . . 0 points
	<div align="right">Points_____</div>

How do you feel about the rate of inflation and the effect it may have on your retirement income?	☐ I would like my investment earnings to keep
	   up with the rate of inflation, but I don't
	   want to take chances losing money. . . . . . . 0 points
	☐ I would like my investment earnings to earn more
	   than the rate of inflation over the long run, even
	   though there's some risk that my investments
	   may lose money in the short-term . . . . 7 points
	☐ I would like my investment earnings to earn much
	   more than the rate of inflation over the long run,
	   even though there's a greater risk that my
	   investments may lose money in the
	   short-term. . . . . 14 points
	<div align="right">Points_____</div>

Investor Profile Questionnaire, *continued*

My feelings about risk can be summed up as:	☐ I want the most opportunity for long-term growth in my retirement account, and I'm comfortable with large ups and downs in the value of my account during the short-term . . . . 14 points ☐ I can accept some daily ups and downs in the value of my retirement account if it means I can potentially earn more over the long run . . . . 7 points ☐ I'd rather accept lower long-term growth than worry about my retirement account losing money . . . . 0 points Points_____

The table at right shows five examples of how much $1,000 invested in a retirement account may go up or down in value after one year. Which investment would make you feel the most comfortable?

	Worst Case	Average Case	Best Case	
Investment 1	$985	$1,060	$1,125	. . . . 0 points
Investment 2	$970	$1,080	$1,190	. . . . 4 points
Investment 3	$910	$1,100	$1,310	. . . . 8 points
Investment 4	$850	$1,120	$1,450	. . . 13 points
Investment 5	$790	$1,140	$1,590	. . . 19 points

Points_____

In how many years do you plan to retire?	☐ 0–2 years . . . . Subtract 20 points ☐ 3–5 years . . . . Subtract 10 points ☐ 6–10 years . . . . Subtract 3 points ☐ Over 10 years . . . . . . 0 points, skip the next question Points_____
Once you retire, how many years do you think you'll need retirement income? You may spend 20 to 30 years of your life in retirement. Withdrawing money over a period of time rather than all at once increases your time horizon.	☐ 0–2 years . . . . Subtract 10 points ☐ 3–5 years . . . . Subtract 5 points ☐ 6–10 years . . . . Subtract 3 points ☐ 11–15 years . . . . Subtract 1 point ☐ more than 15 years . . . . 0 points Points_____
Your total points determine which Investment Risk Profile best matches your level of investment comfort.	TOTAL POINTS PROFILE O 0–21 points Income (Very Conservative Risk Taker) O 22–40 points Income & Growth (Conservative) O 41–59 points Growth & Income (Slightly conservative) O 60–78 points Growth (Moderate) O 79–100 points Aggressive Growth (Aggressive)

ANOTHER PERSPECTIVE ON RISK LEVELS

I (Larry) think that Ron and his firm do an excellent job with identifying risk tolerance levels of their clients, using questionnaires similar to the one on the previous page. I would like to add an anecdotal approach to defining risk levels.

I have observed that the more income people have at their disposal, the less cautious they are with it. Some years ago I did an informal survey of higher income doctors and business owners I knew to determine how many of them had lost money in a bad investment. I was astounded to discover that 100 percent of those surveyed had made at least one bad investment.

Next, I surveyed some middle-income families I had counseled and found that about 50 percent of them had lost money in a bad investment. Finally, I surveyed average-income families. Of this group about 10 percent had lost money through a bad investment.

The logical conclusion you could draw is that those in the lower income group had less money to risk so they obviously would have made fewer investments. Not so. The percentage of investments made stayed remarkably constant, regardless of the income. But the kinds of investments they chose and risks they assumed changed drastically, depending on their incomes.

My conclusion is that the lower income investors are less willing to assume high risks. The higher income investors willingly accept the greater risks. Probably much of this can be explained by what is called "sweat equity." In other words, the lower the income, the more sweat went into the money to be risked. Perhaps the lesson to be learned from this survey is to treat all of your money as if you earned it by chopping firewood for a living.

STEP 2: MAKE A PLAN

Begin planning your portfolio by evaluating your current asset allocation (the percentage of your holdings invested in various asset classes). Record your findings under the "Current" column in this chart.

Asset Class and Category	Current ($ Amount) (% of Portfolio)	Desired Category ($ Amount) (% of Portfolio)
U.S. Stocks		
Large Cap		
Small Cap		
International Stocks		
Developed		
Developing		
Bonds		
Short-Term		
Intermediate		
Real Estate		
Real Estate Stocks		
Precious Metals		
Total		

Using the results from the risk-tolerance assessment on the Investor Profile Questionnaire, you can establish a portfolio goal that complements your investment temperament. The next figure illustrates how a portfolio might be structured, depending on the risk tolerance of a particular investor.

	Income	Income & Growth	Growth & Income	Growth	Aggressive Growth
U.S. Stocks					
Large Company	15%	20%	25%	30%	20%
Small Company			10%	15%	20%
International Stocks					
Developed Markets	5%	10%	10%	10%	15%
Developing Markets			5%	5%	10%
Bonds					
Short-Term	45%	40%	20%	15%	10%
Intermediate Term	30%	25%	20%	15%	10%
Real Estate					
Real Estate Stocks			5%	5%	10%
Precious Metals	5%	5%	5%	5%	5%
TOTAL	100%	100%	100%	100%	100%

STEP 3: BUY AND SELL

Once you have decided how to allocate assets for your investment portfolio, you may need to sell some of your current investments in order to reinvest the funds in a different asset and maintain your desired allocation percentages.

STEP 4: MONITOR

The final stage in building your portfolio is monitoring. Review your investment accounts regularly, perhaps on a quarterly or semiannual basis. Remember that your portfolio is structured according to a carefully developed plan. Market swings should not make you want to buy or sell. Also, your asset allocation percentages should remain fairly constant, and you will periodically need to rebalance your portfolio.

Rebalancing a portfolio involves simply noting where growth and erosion have occurred and making corrections. For example, suppose your asset allocation plan reflects a mix of 65 percent stocks and 35 percent bonds. If the stock market improves and the bond market declines, you may wind up at the end of a quarter with 72 percent of your assets in stocks and 28 percent in bonds. Rebalancing means selling the extra 7 percent in stocks and buying it back in bonds. (Interestingly enough, rebalancing is one of the best ways to actually buy low and sell high!)

How often should you rebalance? There is no precise answer. We would recommend at least annually but perhaps as often as quarterly. A monthly rebalancing is too frequent.

Many people age fifty and over failed to rebalance their portfolios during the great stock market run of the late 1990s and then later suffered the consequences. Large-company growth stocks, particularly in the U.S., outperformed other asset classes for four years in a row from 1995 to 1998. Many near-retirees began to realize that they could retire sooner if this pace continued. Many may have thought, *Why keep some in this bond fund or international fund when the U.S. growth stocks are doing so well?*

When the markets declined from 2000 to 2002, the U.S. growth stocks suffered the most. Bond funds were up during each of those three years. Rebalancing takes discipline, but it reestablishes the original allocation and helps to minimize losses.

A FEW FINAL WORDS ABOUT INVESTMENTS AND DIVERSIFICATION

Diversification reduces risk. It does not offer the greatest potential return or offer a guaranteed return. The mantra in the financial planning community is: "To build wealth, concentrate; to preserve wealth, diversify."

To achieve the greatest amount of wealth, a person should concentrate. Bill Gates built his wealth by concentrating his portfolio on Microsoft; Sam Walton, on Wal-Mart. To keep their billions, these men had regular programs to sell company stock and diversify in order to preserve their wealth. You may not have the wealth of the *Forbes* 400 richest people; but as you grow older, you will need to diversify to preserve your wealth.

Although we did not include it in the Diversification Hierarchy, another area to diversify is "away from your employer." This means to invest your 401(k) or stock portfolio in other companies besides your employer. The goal here is to reduce risk. You are already dependent on your employer for your current earnings, health insurance, and pension. Why tie up more of your wealth by investing in company stock? Talk to an employee of a company that unexpectedly went bankrupt. That employee will confirm our recommendation.

The challenging balance is to reduce risk as one ages but to maintain investments that will grow and surpass inflation. We like what Peter Lynch, former mutual fund manager of Fidelity Magellan Fund, said in his book *Beating the Street:*

> Whatever method you use to pick stocks or stock mutual funds, your ultimate success or failure will depend on your ability to ignore the worries of the world long enough to allow your investments to succeed. It isn't the head but the stomach that determines the fate of the stock picker. It's your behavior after selecting the assets.[1]

No matter who you are, you will make investment mistakes. We have made them too. If you have experienced market losses, then learn from it, move on, and forget it. Too often we beat ourselves up over bad decisions. Or our spouses don't forget, or won't let us forget, our mistakes. Just as God forgives us for our sins, including poor stewardship, we should forgive our spouses and ourselves as well.

Preserving your investments and creating an income stream to last is important. But even more important is what you keep after your expenses. It doesn't matter what you make but what is left after the expenses. We will focus on spending in the next chapter.

ASK RON

Q. I am in my late fifties. A nice fellow at church has been talking to me about a fixed deferred annuity. The guaranteed interest sounds pretty good in this market environment because my mutual funds have not done well recently. Should I purchase the annuity?

A. I am not trying to be evasive, but that is the wrong approach. Buying the annuity may be the answer, but the answer to your question should not be driven by the market today. If so, then the answer is going to change a few years from now.

What should drive your investment decision? The answers to two questions: What are your long-term goals? And what is your risk tolerance? After you answer these questions, then you can determine what investment vehicles to use. Many people fall into a binary trap by asking the question: Should I do this or not? That is the wrong question. Ask the wrong question or ask a question the wrong way, and you will get the wrong answer. Better questions to ask are, "Do I need to reevaluate my risk tolerance?" or, "Do I need to rebalance my portfolio?"

Q. During the stock market's downturn from 2000 to 2002, did you make substantial changes to your investment portfolio?

A. No. I did not change my allocation or sell out of any investments recently. As I sit here today, my investments are down 15 to 20 percent at the end of 2002. But I don't anticipate doing anything with those investments for the next fifteen years. The fact that they are down is just a piece of information at this point in time. As we mentioned in the chapter, I have to go back to my original plan: What is my ultimate use of the money? When do I anticipate needing it? Do I have a long-term perspective?

Back in October 1987, I was watching the television news coverage of reactions after the biggest one-day point drop in stock market history.

The report had included several people responding with the expected panic and hysteria. A reporter approached a woman in her late fifties and asked, "Are you an investor?"

"Yes," came her controlled reply.

The reporter inquired, "How are you reacting?"

"I'm finding it pretty entertaining. I have no intention of selling. The market being down today is simply a piece of information to me. In fact, if I could buy, I would buy now."

That woman had the right long-term perspective. Also, I might add, her portfolio greatly benefited over subsequent years if she stayed with her plan.

Q. How do you see the stock market performing throughout the rest of the first decade of the 2000s?

A. Sorry to disappoint you and any other readers looking for a prediction, but I have no idea. I guess my basic philosophy is that I can't see the future and I have trouble trying to predict it. That is why we wrote this chapter on investments with a focus on principles. My advice is to make investment decisions based on principles, no matter what the future is.

I will add, though, that I think you should continue to invest in the stock market. Many over age fifty have been spooked by the declines of the stock market in the early 2000s. They then have sold out of the stock market. But this could be a mistake.

As we mentioned in chapter 5 about the enemy of inflation, your investment returns need to outpace inflation to provide you a "real" return. Over various long-term periods of our nation's history, the stock market gives you the best opportunity to beat inflation. As a recent advertisement by the mutual fund company Oppenheimer Funds says, "There are two times when people forget their investment principles. At the top of the market and at the bottom."

Q. My husband and I have discussed how to invest the rollover of my husband's 401(k) from his previous employer. We have read about investing according to one's "risk tolerance." That's our problem: my husband is a much more aggressive investor, and I am very conservative. Technically, it is his 401(k), but we see it as ours because we chose for me to stay at home. How do we decide our combined risk tolerance?

A. To me, it is a decision for both of you. In our firm we don't recommend distinguishing between his and hers.

I say in almost every one of my books that God did not give you a spouse to frustrate you but to complete you. The reality is that you and your husband will think, react, and plan differently. That's a good thing. You can balance each other out. You and your husband should avoid creating a win/lose situation with your financial decisions. You both can discuss and pray about this decision. I think you will end up somewhere in between, which is probably a good balance.

ASK LARRY

Q. Larry, we have a surplus to invest. We already have some mutual fund investments through our IRA. We are considering purchasing residential rental property. What are some things we should consider before buying rental property as an investment?

A. Whether to invest in rental property will depend on your goals and your present financial structure. If you are comfortable with handling real estate and rental property, I believe it can be an attractive investment and a portion of a balanced investment portfolio. Try to have equity in it, an ideal location for rental property, and enough cash flow in your own budget to carry the additional payments during the times it is not rented.

Even in a bad economy people need somewhere to live, but include in your cash flow calculations the possibility of the property being vacant for a month or two or rent decreasing. Decide if it will be an ideal long-term holding for you and your temperament. If it is, then hang on to it and even begin to prepay the current amortized mortgage against it. The more equity you have in rental property, the more likely the value of the property will never drop below the loan value on the property if real estate plummets again.

I think rental housing is one of the soundest areas of investing for the average family, but it is perhaps the most difficult area because it requires a lot of work. Your mutual fund investment portfolio will never call you on the coldest night of the year to say that the plumbing is stopped up and will never leave a mess to clean up after vacating. Here are a few other specific considerations: (1) Look for residential housing in a good rental area. (2) Be certain your rental house is a fair deal for the renters and for you. (3) Be sure your personality is conducive to being a landlord. (4) Have enough equity to ensure a good cash flow.

If you can do most of the maintenance yourself, then your chances to realize a profit improve. The major disadvantage of rental property is the aggravation factor resulting from repairs and late payments (or nonpayment) from renters. The advantages to owning rental housing include these: you receive some tax advantages on your income tax; the rental payments can retire the loan on the house (someone else making your payments); and rental housing is virtually inflation proof.

Q. What are some personal examples of your investment successes and failures?

A. I often say on my radio programs, "Don't take my advice on specific investments. I am not very good at it."

My wife, Judy, and I can now laugh about one of those bad decisions. In the 1960s and early 1970s, we lived in central Florida. We had only about $500 to invest. Judy had heard about this thing called Disney World. It was going to build some park and open in Orlando. She suggested that we buy some of Disney's stock.

With all my wisdom and insight, I said, "No way can something like that survive. It's stupid to open up something like that in the middle of nowhere. There's too much swampy land, and besides, it's too hot."

Because my background was in engineering, I overruled and bought $500 of Symmetrics Engineering. That company folded many years ago. What would the $500 of Disney stock be worth now? I don't want to know.

On a more positive note, I reduced my stock holdings substantially—down to 30 percent of my portfolio—by selling stocks in 1998 and 1999. I followed through on my warnings about the stock market being over-valued as I wrote about in my book *Crisis Control*.

But more urgently for me, my decision was also based on my personal situation—a diagnosis of cancer. My health condition forced me to look at my investing-time horizon like an eighty-five-year-old man. Someone at that age should have little in the stock market, so I reduced my stock holdings. I used some appreciated stocks to do my charitable giving. I missed some gains in 1998 and 1999, but I missed the downfall of the market from 2000 to 2002. I moved out of the stock market to income-oriented investments to support my wife in case I died.

ASK YOURSELF

- What are my reasons for investing?
- Am I sometimes tempted with worldly motives for investing? Which ones?
- Do I have a lower risk tolerance as I have grown older? Does the allocation of my portfolio reflect my current risk tolerance?
- Am I adequately diversified from my employer? To reduce risk, have I minimized my holdings of my employer's stock?
- Have I been monitoring and rebalancing my portfolio?

CHAPTER 7

SPEND TO LAST

— OR —

"Money Talks . . . But All Mine Ever Says Is Good-bye"

Despite the high cost of living, it's still popular.
ANONYMOUS

Almost any man knows how to earn money, but not one in a million
knows how to spend it.
HENRY DAVID THOREAU

We are not to judge thrift solely by the test of saving or spending. If
one spends what he should prudently save, that certainly is to be
deplored. But if one saves what he should prudently spend, that is not
necessarily to be commended. A wise balance between the two is the
desired end.
OWEN D. YOUNG

Know well the condition of your flocks,
And pay attention to your herds.
PROVERBS 27:23

There is precious treasure and oil in the dwelling of the wise,
But a foolish man swallows it up.
PROVERBS 21:20

W hen I (Ron) speak to Christian groups, I occasionally encounter people who say they are counting on the rapture to get them out of debt. Usually, such comments are made with tongue firmly planted in cheek, although sometimes I suspect they reflect a genuine philosophy!

I like to point out Psalm 37:21: *"The wicked borrows and does not pay back."* I often follow this reference with a question: What if Jesus only raptures those who are debt-free? This thought typically elicits a cough of nervous laughter from the crowd.

"You know," I then jokingly wonder aloud, "the rapture may have already occurred!"

Our nation often treats debt with jokes or a shoulder-shrugging attitude. This nonchalant attitude is one of the reasons our government and the average U.S. consumer have so much debt!

Debt exists because you spend more than you earn. Therefore, debt is a symptom of a spending problem. Many of our other books have focused on budgeting, spending, and living without debt.

Spending choices play a vital role in making your wealth last. Spending and lifestyle choices are interrelated with the previous two chapters. Your level of income sets (or should set) the upper limit on your spending. The relationship of your spending to your income will help determine if your investments will last and remain as investments.

We are thankful to God that we have been able to write and speak about spending topics without being pummeled by stones. We understand that telling people how to spend, or limit spending, their money is not popular. Most people enjoy spending money, and most people hate being told what to do.

Well, relax just a bit. We will not tell you where to spend every dime of your budget. We will discuss the overall need to control spending. We will also discuss unique spending challenges for those over fifty.

Ultimately, spending decisions are up to you. You alone can make decisions, such as whether to cut back on your tool collection or eating out at restaurants.

WHY SPENDING STILL MATTERS TO THE OVER-FIFTY CROWD

Bob and Dora, in their mid-fifties, currently enjoy more discretionary income than ever before in their lives. Bob has reached his peak career earnings as a senior manager. Dora returned to the workforce as a teacher after their children completed college.

As an empty-nest couple, they have no orthodontics bills to pay, no ballet or piano lessons to fund, and, best of all, no young male drivers on their car insurance policies. Like many of their peers in their Sunday school class, they have more income, more time, and less debt.

When Bob reviewed his year-end savings statements and investment accounts, he was surprised that he and Dora had not saved more. He is putting away more in his 401(k) at work, but it seems their surplus is not as big as he expected. He would have thought that their income level would allow them to save even more and finish paying off the mortgage sooner.

People in their fifties still have to watch their spending habits, precisely because they have more income. There is an old saying that an increase in pay is the first step toward bankruptcy. It is so easy to spend away all the income increases, so simple to find new ways to spend when expenses decrease.

After the expenses of raising children and perhaps assisting them through college, it is the best time to build savings and pay off debt. During their fifties, people are in the best stage to prepare for their later years.

HOW DO YOU MONITOR AND PLAN YOUR SPENDING?

A budget! A budget is not the goal of your finances; it is a tool to help you reach your financial goals. We think it is the most effective tool to understanding and managing the financial resources God gives you.

The word *budget* scares many people. Perhaps they see budgeting as a punishment plan or an impossible task. It does not have to be that way. A budget is simply a spending plan for your family. It maximizes your family finances so that you can be more effective for God both spiritually and financially. A budget is a catalyst for good communication in an area often characterized by conflict.

After describing the need for a budget on the radio, at seminars, and in books, we sense that many still resist budgeting. To help you win the battle of your mind, use the following list of truths, originally published in Larry's *Family Financial Workbook,* to overcome the common myths of budgeting.

BUDGETING: MYTHS AND TRUTHS

Myth: We tried a budget once before, and it didn't work.

Truth: We don't perfect new skills on the first try. Did you ride a bike, cook a gourmet meal, or hit a home run the first time you tried? If you have tried budgeting previously, you are in the best position to succeed. You can learn from your previous mistakes and experience. You know it takes effort and can be determined to make a lasting change.

Myth: We live on a variable income and, therefore, cannot budget.

Truth: More than anyone, people on a variable income should budget. Although your income varies, you still need to follow a budget to ensure your expenses do not exceed your average variable income.

Myth: It is impossible to budget for contingencies and unplanned expenses.

Truth: Contingencies are one of the most important items to include in your budget. Although you may not know exactly what will happen, you know that some doctor visits and car repairs will happen. The sooner you begin your budget and establish some history and experience, the better you can predict future occurrences. Companies estimate contingencies. An entire industry (insurance) is built around estimating contingencies. Build contingencies into your budget.

Myth: We are not mathematically inclined.

Truth: A budget does not involve calculus, geometry, or complex algebraic equations. Knowing addition and subtraction is enough. Other tools exist, such as the calculator or computer, to eliminate any math that may be difficult or tedious.

Myth: We are not financial types.

Truth: Although the budget is the most basic and important financial tool, you do not need a business degree, stock market knowledge, or an accounting background to establish a budget. You are simply keeping track of the money coming in and going out.

Myth: We don't earn enough income to budget.

Truth: You definitely need a budget. The smaller your income, the stronger your need for a budget. When you budget, you limit excess spending, and it's as if your income grows.

Myth: We earn too much income to worry about a budget.

Truth: Although you may be blessed with an above-average income, a budget can help you be a good steward with your surplus. Unfortunately, as incomes rise, the expenses rise at the same or greater rate. Setting a plan and keeping a budget will help you use your growing income for the benefit of your family and others.

Myth: We have money problems because we don't have enough income.

Truth: Usually, financial problems result from overspending. Budgeting can help you see the areas where spending may be out of control.

Myth: We don't have time to keep track of a budget.

Truth: It takes far more time to handle a financial mess than it does to keep your finances in order. Remember that an ounce of prevention is worth a pound of cure. Keeping a budget takes less time than you think. After you establish your budget, it takes only thirty minutes to an hour per week to maintain it.

ADJUSTING SPENDING TO THE RETIREMENT (TRANSITION) PHASE

Besides limiting spending so that you can save more during the peak earning years, you also should monitor your spending as you transition to retirement. This is practice time.

We have observed that many people think they can cut their income at retirement by 25 to 50 percent and live just fine. However, those living expenses just do not go down as easily as people think. Conventional wisdom does hold that living expenses decrease after retirement. But as with most generalities, it depends. Expenses may stay the same or even increase, depending on your lifestyle choices, health needs, and family support.

Financial planners have long said that retirement expenses should be about 70 to 80 percent of your total expenses before retirement. That's one of those general rules that may or may not apply to you. You cannot simply assume that your living expenses will go down. Some will, but others will increase.

Expenses that usually decrease after retirement:

Payroll tax (FICA, Medicare)

Local payroll withholding taxes

401(k) contributions or other retirement plan contributions

Commuting expenses

Work-related expenses (office gifts, lunches, new clothing)

Giving (if a decrease in income occurred)

Expenses that usually increase after retirement:

Medical insurance

Prescription drugs

Travel and vacation expenses

Entertainment (eating out, golf, recreation)

Hobby expenses

Expenses unaffected by retirement:

    Utilities

    Home repairs

    Groceries

    Mortgage payment

    Gifts

    Insurance for home, auto, liability

We recommend that you make any lifestyle and spending adjustments at least one year *before* retirement. We have observed that if you haven't made spending adjustments before retirement, then you are not going to be able to make any adjustments suddenly at retirement.

In addition to using a budget and adjusting your lifestyle and spending level, we want to discuss specific spending categories that may pose new challenges at this stage of your life.

HELPING ADULT CHILDREN

Al and Betty, empty-nested for five years, were just starting to get ahead financially in their late fifties. They had finished paying for college and weddings. Their children were on their own, beginning their families.

All of this changed for Al and Betty with the surprise late-night appearance of their pregnant daughter and two-year-old grandson at their back door. Their daughter's young husband left her with one child and one on the way. He also left her with credit card bills and no home. Like most caring parents, Al and Betty welcomed them and supported them for the next year.

Rick and Marlene, peers of Al and Betty, have a different situation with their twenty-eight-year-old son. He has held various jobs, most of which paid well. But he usually finds a way to waste his money. He continues to live at home. From his perspective, why not? He gets free food, free laundry, and free rent. He even receives an occasional bailing out of his credit card debt by his father.

How much should we help our adult children financially? You must maintain a balance of helping with needs but without taking away their motivation to provide for themselves.

If your children have a basic need—food, clothing, or shelter—as a result of circumstances beyond their control (loss of employment, sickness, inadequate income, or disaster), helping them temporarily is certainly reasonable. Al and Betty had the means, and their daughter was in the midst of a crisis with legitimate financial needs.

However, if the financial crisis was caused by mismanagement of funds, parents need to show tough love. Rick and Marlene need some more backbone in dealing with their son. They need to let him know that, although they love him, any financial help must be contingent on his establishing a workable budget and getting good financial and budgeting counsel.

It is never too late to begin teaching your children about finances, particularly God's principles of handling money. If you find that your grown children are having financial difficulties, use this as an opportunity to help them get good counsel. Too many parents attempt to buffer their children financially, but that usually makes the problem worse. Don't give your children more than they can handle, and don't co-sign loans for them.

Sometimes we have to take upon ourselves the role that God has often taken with His own people. He would exile them for a period of time to help them understand their responsibilities. There are times when God allows problems to come into our lives and withholds finances to increase our dependence on Him. He does this to strengthen us. *"All discipline for the moment seems not to be joyful, but sorrowful; yet to those who have been trained by it, afterwards it yields the peaceful fruit of righteousness"* (Hebrews 12:11).

Even though we are called by God to be teachers of our children, we are not responsible for the decisions they make as adults. Sometimes we must allow them to fail. Proverbs 16:26 says, *"A worker's appetite works for him, for his hunger urges him on."* Some of life's most valuable lessons are learned because of trying and failing. Love your children enough to allow them to fail. This can be difficult, so you must set your will to do it, not allowing your emotions to sway you.

Crown Financial Ministries has volunteer budget counselors throughout the country who offer their services at no charge to people who desire to establish budgets, get out of debt, and honor God through their finances. The budget counselors, ministering under the authority of their local churches, have been trained in godly principles of finance to help people become worthy stewards of the resources God has entrusted to their care. If your adult children desire this kind of financial counsel, tell them to send a written request to the counseling department at Crown Financial Ministries, 601 Broad St SE, Gainesville GA 30501. Crown will then send them the name of the nearest Crown volunteer budget counselor in their area.

Spoiling or Blessing Grandchildren?

What grandparent doesn't like to do a little grandchild spoiling? However, there are several things you may consider when dealing with your grandchildren. Foremost is the ruling guide never to usurp the authority of the children's parents, often one of the most difficult things for a grandparent.

Barb says that she works in her part-time job just to earn money to buy things for her grandchildren. Barb's son thinks that his kids already have too many toys. He says his kids are in the habit of expecting a present every time Barb sees them. Barb should respect her son's opinions as the authority over his children. Perhaps she could redirect her generosity toward buying needed shoes or beginning a college savings fund rather than toys.

As grandparents, you have wisdom that is worth far more than toys. Teach your grandchildren the blessing of knowing and loving God rather than knowing only the latest cartoon character. Give them experiences and memories through quality time rather than stuff.

Exercise self-control—another tough one for any grandparent. There's no better way to help your children establish financial discipline in their children than by your being well-balanced in this area. Then, as soon as they are old enough to begin to receive money, you can encourage them to give the money to God by tithing first.

Grandparents need not only to teach but also to practice moderation, regardless of their ability to generate income. As a grandparent, you can do more for your children and your grandchildren by following God's instructions and exercising discipline in your lifestyle than by all the financial gifts you might be able to lavish on them.

Finally, every grandparent (and parent) should remember that a *little* bit of grandchild spoiling never hurt anyone.

RECREATIONAL VEHICLES

Perhaps you have dreams of traveling in retirement. You may want to be free to see the country. As retirement nears, you may be tempted like others to begin to look at something you have never looked at before in your life: a recreational vehicle or motor home. Perhaps a friend bought one, or perhaps the thought struck you as you drove behind one on the interstate.

On occasion, someone asks us if it is good stewardship to buy an RV. There is not a one-size-fits-all answer because it is an individual answer. Some couples who are healthy and enjoy traveling love their RVs. Some couples actually sell their homes and live in their RVs full-time, visiting family members, friends, and even donating time to ministries. On the other hand, some couples have spent thousands of dollars for RVs with all the bells and whistles only to discover that they really didn't like spending all their vacation time on the road in such cramped quarters.

First, you need to decide whether an RV fits into the category of a need, a want, or a desire. Even if it's "merely" a desire, that doesn't necessarily mean you shouldn't have one. After all, God does say that if we delight ourselves in Him, He will give us the desires of our hearts (see Psalm 37:4).

Next, you have to consider your budget. Can you pay for an RV in cash, or will you have to borrow the money? We strongly urge that you do not borrow the money for an RV. Be prepared; you will likely spend more on an RV than your first house.

Third, will you buy a new or a used RV? Since new vehicles of any kind depreciate by about 25 percent the minute you drive them off the dealer's lot, it might be wiser to buy a reliable used RV.

Another option would be to rent an RV and travel in it for a week or two. This will give you a good idea of whether you like it without the commitment of ownership. In fact, if you contemplate using an RV for only a few weeks each year, renting one whenever you need it could be far more cost effective than buying one. You must like the RV life because they rarely make financial sense. You could stay in nice hotels for a few years consecutively for what an RV costs to buy, not to mention the high gas costs.

RVs *can* be like exercise equipment—often bought but seldom used. It might be better to err on the side of caution—that is, rent before you buy.

RETIREMENT COMMUNITIES AND ASSISTED-LIVING CENTERS

Terms like *retirement community* and *assisted living* are becoming more familiar to most of us, but the concepts are not always clear.

A retirement community is usually a separate development of houses, town houses, or condominiums with low-maintenance yards. There are usually age restrictions, such as sixty-two, and family restrictions, such as no young children. Residents share certain amenities, such as a pool, tennis courts, and community buildings.

Deciding to move to a retirement community is a personal decision. It's wise to plan ahead, and it helps to know your options and make your choices before a situation such as changing health needs forces a decision. Often people delay the decision of where they want to live because they don't want to deal with the hassle of moving. However, a move won't be any easier five or ten years down the road.

Some people like the idea of a retirement community because they like the security a community setting offers, as well as the companionship of other older adults. Others are ready to get rid of time-consuming lawn work, or they desire more recreation.

There is a range of methods by which a person "buys into" a retirement community. In some communities, ownership is more like a lease than true ownership. Different types of leases often are available. With a refundable lease, a percentage of your deposit is returned, based on the amount of time you have lived in your home, generally with some minimum percentage refund guaranteed.

There are drawbacks to these living arrangements. The initial costs are often higher than other forms of home ownership. Then the high monthly maintenance fees generate the feeling that you will never have a paid-for home. After a period of time, some residents say that they miss

It may be that by the witness of your life and by caring for your parents' physical needs, they may come to know the Lord. Is it possible that God has brought them to this point for just such a time as this? Which is more important, the amount of money you will have to spend in order to help your parents or your parents' salvation?

Supporting your aging parents is a multifaceted decision and more complex than we can adequately cover. We would recommend a book published by Focus on the Family called *Complete Guide to Caring for Aging Loved Ones*.

Financial support is an important way to help your parents. There may be additional ways to help and honor your parents besides providing money.

- Provide financial and investment advice. Help them steer clear of schemes and telemarketing pitches. Offer to read over contracts or commitments containing fine print. Introduce them to your financial adviser or lawyer. Give recommendations for professional counsel or attend meetings with them.

- Provide repairs, cleaning, or maintenance. Change the oil, clean the house, mow the yard, clean the gutters, or put things in the attic.

- Be sensitive to the fears of helplessness your parents may have as a result of changes in health and abilities. Give them your support, not interference.

- Encourage and allow them to make their own decisions. You have more influence than authority with them. Remember that parents are like you and your own children: they resent being told what to do.

- Listen. Generally, parents are willing to offer advice to you. Even as an adult, you are to respect and hear them. If you do, then you have earned the privilege to turn the discussion to *their* situation.

- Keep them in your home. Although this option may not always be practical, due to either your living circumstance or your parents' condition, be open to this solution. Related to this topic, we heard the following story, called "The Tale of the Wooden Bowl." It reminds us of the concept of honoring parents.

A frail, old man went to live with his son, daughter-in-law, and four-year-old grandson.

The old man's hands trembled, his eyesight blurred, and his step faltered. During the nightly family dinner together, the elderly grandfather's shaky hands and failing sight made eating difficult. Peas rolled off his spoon onto the floor. When he tried to grasp the glass, milk spilled on the tablecloth.

The son and daughter-in-law became irritated with the regular messes. "We must do something about Grandfather," said the son. "I've had enough of his spilled milk, noisy eating, and food on the floor."

The husband and wife decided to set a small table in the corner. There, Grandfather ate alone while the rest of the family enjoyed dinner at the table. Since Grandfather had broken a dish or two, his food was served in a wooden bowl.

When the family glanced in Grandfather's direction, sometimes he had a tear in his eyes as he sat alone. Still the only words the couple had for him were sharp admonitions when he dropped a fork or spilled food. The four-year-old watched it all in silence.

One evening, before supper, the father noticed his son playing with wood scraps on the floor. He asked the child sweetly, "What are you making?"

Just as sweetly, the boy responded, "Oh, I am making a little bowl for you and Mama to eat your food in when I grow up."

The little boy smiled and went back to work.

The words so struck the parents that they were speechless. Then tears started to stream down their cheeks. Though no words were spoken, both knew what must be done. That evening, the husband took Grandfather's hand and gently led him back to the family table.

For the remainder of his days, he had every meal with the family. For some reason, neither husband nor wife seemed to care any longer when a fork was dropped, milk was spilled, or the tablecloth was soiled.

To the best of your human abilities, love your parents, pray for them, and meet their needs as required through the Word. It may not be the easiest principle to follow, but it is God's principle that you are to honor your father and your mother regardless of their actions.

You may think that we left out one of the biggest components of your budget: health insurance. Well, you are right. We left it out of this chapter but not out of this book. It is so important that we devoted the next chapter to it and other types of insurance.

ASK RON

Q. Have you helped your children with paying for their houses?

A. Yes. Although helping them in this way is not a biblical mandate, my wife and I were able to help them and chose to do so.

Our approach, however, was different from the usual giving of money for a down payment. We waited until our adult children and spouses saved their own money for a down payment. They selected the home they wanted, they chose the mortgage option they wanted, and they settled on a monthly payment they could afford. Then we surprised them with a monthly gift to them to help pay down the principal on their mortgage.

Our approach doesn't affect their lifestyle, doesn't help them live beyond their means, and doesn't involve surety on our part. We enjoy helping them now but without keeping them dependent on us. We can stop at any time.

ASK LARRY

Q. Do you still keep a budget? If so, why?

A. Yes, I do. Although we do not have debt and generally have a surplus, we have found that a budget remains a useful tool. It helps us to keep track and gives a record to see how and where we have spent money over the years.

It also helps control what I call "creeping spending inflation." Like the fictitious couple, Bob and Dora, in this chapter, it is easy for spending to go up in step with increases in income. Then you can be left wondering, "Where did it all go?"

ASK RON

Q. Do you still maintain a budget for your family? If so, why?

A. Yes. We have found our spending habits are pretty well set, but we still budget. We don't really budget from the standpoint of having to control every dollar. But we use our budget to be aware of where, over time, we might be tempted to overspend. Typically, we are well within our budget every year just because we budget conservatively.

One of the things Judy and I have the opportunity to do is to sit down periodically and ask ourselves the question: "Are we spending money where we want to spend money?" That's a very good exercise to go through.

ASK LARRY

Q. We have two children in college. They don't manage their money very well and have had some failures being on their own in another town. They think that my husband and I have no money problems and that such money struggles only happen when in college. Can we still teach them at this age? Have you experienced anything similar?

A. Because they are no longer young kids, begin to be more open with them about your finances. Let them know failures you have had and allow them to observe your financial struggles.

I experienced such a challenge when one of my sons came home from college to ask me for help in clearing up his checking account.

He had eight checks overdrawn and seventy dollars in overdraft charges. Needless to say, I was discouraged. The only thing worse for a Christian financial counselor would be for my own account to be overdrawn, which happened once when I forgot to make a deposit.

God used my son's problem to help me realize that just because I teach financial discipline doesn't mean my children understand it. I was able to share why financial principles are in God's Word. First, set an example; then, lead and encourage your children.

ASK RON

Q. In what areas do you see the over-fifty crowd going overboard on their spending?

A. Probably in the areas of leisure and recreation. I think it is a spiritual issue. It comes back to the philosophy so many have accepted that it's OK to retire to a life of pleasure and comfort. It certainly is attractive when you are in the midst of being worn out and wishing to enjoy the fruit of your labor.

Judy and I have been dealing with this issue. Several years ago we bought a second home as a place to get away. We have spent some time there, but what we have found is that the resort environment, the atmosphere, and the people are all in an amusement and retirement mode.

We stepped back after a few years and said, "We are not sure this represents our value system." It's been a hard decision because we do enjoy it. We are not saying that second homes are sinful or wrong, but we found the experience was not in line with what God wanted us to do. As of right now, we plan to sell that home.

ASK YOURSELF

- What categories of spending will I need to adjust as I grow older if my income declines?
- Am I helping or hurting my adult children in the way that I financially give to them?
- If I continue to own my home, will it be serving me in later years, or will I be serving it?
- What other people may depend on me as I grow older?
- What physical or medical disabilities may require significant levels of spending as my spouse and I grow older?
- Have I discussed with my spouse the amount of time and money we have available for supporting aging parents?

CHAPTER 8

INSURANCE FOR
WEALTH TO LAST

— OR —

"Life Begins at Fifty:
Unfortunately Everything Else
Wears Out, Spreads Out, or
Falls Out!"

I suppose that I shall have to die beyond my means.
OSCAR WILDE (UPON BEING TOLD THE COST OF AN OPERATION)

Pray as if everything depended upon God and work as if everything
depended upon man.
FRANCIS CARDINAL SPELLMAN

Call on God, but row away from the rocks.
INDIAN PROVERB

A prudent man sees evil and hides himself,
The naïve proceed and pay the penalty.
PROVERBS 27:12

H——— er husband and college-aged kids began to notice that Ellen occasionally forgot some routine things. Then, they had a few good laughs when she absentmindedly put the mail in the refrigerator. The laughs turned to their worst fears, however, when a doctor diagnosed Ellen with early stages of Alzheimer's disease.

This is the setting to the stirring movie *A Vow to Cherish,* a World Wide Pictures release (a ministry of the Billy Graham Evangelistic Association). John Brighton and his wife, Ellen, are faced with a merciless illness that will either confirm their love or destroy their marriage. Their careers and family are thrown into a tailspin as life becomes more and more desperate for them. It is a compelling story about the power of faith, hope, and true commitment.

Because the film focuses more on marital commitment, it does not provide the details of how the Brighton family survives financially during a long-term illness. This illness resulted in the loss of one income, Ellen's teaching position. Was there any disability insurance? How was that income replaced?

She underwent many tests and procedures. Did they have adequate health insurance? Was the health insurance through his job or her job? If it was from her job, how was her health insurance affected by not returning to work?

With no physical ailments, only mental, she would likely live many more years but still need at-home care. Most health insurance policies will not pay for ongoing long-term care in a nursing home or at home. Was there any long-term care insurance? If John was going to care for her at home, how would he continue to earn a living? How would he pay for full-time home health care assistance?

Whew! Life is complicated, and insurance seems to add complication to it. Insurance can enable you to survive financially through the unexpected storms life brings. But choosing the right kind and the right amounts of insurance can be overwhelming. Things used to be a lot simpler back when doctors made home visits and were paid with farm produce, midwives helped birth babies at home, and Uncle Charlie fashioned Uncle Bob's coffin in his carpentry shop.

In this chapter we want to help you identify the basis for insurance, the insurance you can likely do without, and the insurance you most likely will need. An illness like Ellen Brighton's is tragic and unavoidable; the devastating financial consequences are preventable.

INSURANCE—IS IT SCRIPTURAL?

People often ask us two related questions: "Is insurance scriptural?" and, "Does owning insurance reflect a lack of faith?" The answer is both yes and no. Insurance is not specifically defined or mentioned in Scripture; however, the principle of future planning and provision is. *"A prudent man sees evil and hides himself, the naïve proceed and pay the penalty"* (Proverbs 27:12).

Consider insurance as a useful tool to manage risk in the fallen and perverse world in which we live. In simple terms, insurance is a program that lets you pay a little now to cover major expenses in the future due to illness, death, accident, or disaster.

Our nation overall has a balanced court system, but it is also very litigious with many trying to get rich from lawsuits. Therefore, having liability insurance is wise. We have a great health care system deserving of its acclaim, but it is expensive. A life-threatening illness can become "life-savings threatening" without health insurance. *"Be shrewd as serpents, and innocent as doves"* (Matthew 10:16).

Owning insurance does not necessarily reflect a lack of faith in God. Unfortunately, however, one of the negative side effects of relying heavily upon insurance to buffer every little problem is that we also buffer God's guidance. There is no evidence in Scripture that God promises or desires to buffer or protect His people from every difficulty or inconvenience. In fact, conversely, evidence exists that these difficulties are specifically allowed to redirect us or to develop our faith.

Consider the following Scripture passages:

"We also exult in our tribulations, knowing that tribulation brings about perseverance; and perseverance, proven character; and proven character, hope." (Romans 5:3–4)

"That in a great ordeal of affliction their abundance of joy and their deep poverty overflowed in the wealth of their liberality." (2 Corinthians 8:2)

"Consider it all joy, my brethren, when you encounter various trials, knowing that the testing of your faith produces endurance, and let endurance have its perfect result, that you may be perfect and complete, lacking in nothing." (James 1:2–4)

We see from these passages and others in the Bible that God can use trials to strengthen us. Our attitude keeps us in balance. We shouldn't expect insurance to remove any possible negative effects of a sinful world. We shouldn't transfer our trust from God to insurance by using it in excess.

Our attitude should be that insurance is an aid to lower the financial risks of the difficult trials we inevitably will face. It is also a way to provide for our families, as God directs us to do, in the case of our unexpected death. Insurance will never take away pain and suffering. As mentioned previously in this book, I (Larry) was diagnosed with a rare form of cancer in 1995. During this ordeal I have experienced more suffering and trials and questioning than ever before in my life. It has also been a sweet time of knowing God's presence and the prayers of fellow believers. Having health insurance has helped to ease the financial strains on my family from my extensive medical treatments.

INSURANCE MAY DAMAGE YOUR STEWARDSHIP CONSCIENCE

Insurance may provide secondary effects that damage our society, such as greed, slothfulness, waste, and fear. Some have developed an insurance ethic that often rationalizes the cheating of insurance companies. Some committed Christians are willing to use insurance funds to do things they would never consider doing with their own money.

The apparently easy access to insurance company funds promotes an attitude of slothfulness both financially and spiritually: financially because there is less incentive to save and anticipate problems and spiritually because there is less need to pray about future needs of others as well as our own. Those who have access to employer-paid, low-deductible insurance plans have a tendency to forget that not everyone in their communities or churches has the same opportunity.

The misuse of insurance raises its cost and the cost of services covered by insurance. Health care costs us more because few consumers compare prices, and doctors experience longer collection time and increased paperwork. The cost of insurance abuse is passed on to the diligent. Obviously, that discourages conservatism and encourages even more abuses by others. The tendency is to say, "I want to get my fair share too."

WHEN DO YOU NOT NEED INSURANCE?

Insurance companies have thought of every sort of insurance policy imaginable, from pets to credit card theft to contact lenses. Here's our simple test to determine if you need insurance of any kind: Can you provide for an unexpected loss yourself? In essence, can you self-insure? If so, then why use God's resources to pay for an insurance premium?

To think through this further, consider and weigh the answers to the following questions.

> What is the maximum loss exposure?
>
> How likely is that outcome?
>
> How much are the premiums?

Let's say that you are sending a birthday gift in the mail to your grandchild. Your gift costs $60. When paying for the postage, the friendly clerk asks if you want to insure the package for $2.50. You have often said in the past, "Sure, why not." But now you think through the above questions.

1. The maximum loss is $60. You can certainly afford to replace the gift if required.

2. Although the post office sometimes gets bad press, it is very efficient and rarely loses or damages items. The chance of collecting from this insurance is very small.

3. The cost of the insurance seems low at $2.50, but it is a hefty 4 percent of the cost of the gift.

Even though this is a small example, these small amounts added to the costs of many purchases throughout the year add up. If you can insure and afford the risk, then why waste God's resources on something you don't need merely to profit an insurer?

Great emotional appeals can be made for protecting everything from the dishwasher to possible termites. At what point do we say enough? That point has been reached when a Christian looks around and finds that trusting God no longer seems necessary for future material needs. *"And my God will supply all your needs according to His riches in glory in Christ Jesus"* (Philippians 4:19).

You can save thousands of dollars over several years when you use this buying principle: Buy insurance for the big risks; ignore the small risks. Here are some examples of insurance for small risks that you probably don't need:

1. *Home warranty/appliance plans.* Although these are fine if
    a seller of a house buys it for you, you should not buy them
    yourself. Appliances are generally fairly reliable, the costs of
    repairs are usually minor, and these plans often limit the
    coverage on major problems.

2. *Flight insurance.* The selling of flight insurance capitalizes on
    people's fears at the airport. Flying is statistically safer than
    driving. If you need life insurance (see more on this later in the
    chapter), buy adequate life insurance. It will pay if death occurs
    by an airline accident. Flight insurance is relatively expensive.

3. *Cancer insurance.* Another minor insurance policy often
    bought from fear instead of need. Cancer insurance pays a
    fixed-dollar amount to someone diagnosed with cancer. It does
    not pay for the many other diseases or sicknesses possible. If
    you have good health insurance, then it will pay for your med-
    ical bills related to cancer.

4. *Extended warranty and repair plans.* Did you ever notice right
    after a salesperson convinces you of the reliability and quality of
    a new stereo, TV, or computer that the salesperson tries to sell
    you insurance in case it fails? The stores get a large commission
    for selling these policies and aggressively push them. Your new
    item is usually already covered by an original manufacturer's
    warranty, and often the replacement cost is manageable by you.
    Again, self-insure when possible.

5. *Credit life policies.* Direct mail companies, banks, or credit card
    companies push life insurance, or credit life, that pays off your
    loan in case of your death. The premium may appear low because
    the insurance is low and decreases over time as you pay off the
    loan. These policies are expensive for the amount of life insur-
    ance dollars they provide. Get enough life insurance coverage

elsewhere to pay off any debts and avoid these policies (unless you have poor health and can buy these without a medical evaluation).

6. *Auto comprehensive and collision insurance on older vehicles.* Let's say that your ten-year-old vehicle has a book value of $1,500. If it is stolen or totaled from hitting a deer, the insurance company will pay only the book value. If you can afford to replace the car, why pay the extra premium for a small possible payout? If your net worth is very high, you may be able to self-insure newer cars for collision and comprehensive. If you have $500,000 in the bank, do you need to pay premiums for insuring a $20,000 car? You could afford to replace it.

7. *Dental appliances, contact lenses, and eyeglass insurance.* More examples of the endless insurance items that businesses promote. These plans pay if you lose a retainer, tear your contact lenses, or break your glasses. Because these items are relatively inexpensive, just save your money and take the chance.

8. *Pet health care.* Pets can be enjoyable and important parts of your household, but do you really need to insure their health treatment?

9. *Identity theft.* Although identity theft, the stealing of personal information and credit card numbers, is a growing and serious problem, we are not convinced that insurance is necessary or that it can protect you from the inconvenience of this crime. Implement your own forms of prevention. Shred documents with personal information rather than crumpling and throwing them in the trash. Avoid giving personal and credit card information to questionable sources. Review your credit card statements for suspicious activity and report any to the credit card company immediately. Review your credit report annually.

INSURANCE YOU PROBABLY NEED

From a survey by the College of Financial Planning, the following are the top concerns of people within ten years of retirement.

	% Indicating "Much Concern"
1. Financial self-sufficiency/independence	82.2%
2. Meeting health care costs	70.4%
3. Maintaining standard of living	65.9%
4. Provision for long-term care	52.5%

You can address some of these "much concerns" with insurance. For example, long-term care insurance can help provide items 1 and 4. Proper health insurance can help with 1 and 2.

You buy insurance to transfer a risk you are not willing or able to take. You transfer the risk to a company that is willing to assume it for a premium. While many types of insurance are unnecessary, the following types of insurance limit your financial risk and are useful for most people.

Health insurance. We hear from many callers and seminar participants that the reason they continue working in their fifties and sixties is to maintain their health insurance. Besides the other reasons to continue some type of work, we think this is a valid reason to continue employment.

Health insurance is a basic need for those who live in America today. Few families, whether working or retired, can afford the cost of a single hospital stay. A serious illness or long stay in the hospital may cost you more than you paid for your house! Health insurance represents good, logical planning for most of us.

Health insurance and our entire health-care system are too complex to discuss thoroughly in this section of one chapter. Let's keep it simple and straightforward with this advice: Obtain and maintain health insurance. Work at a job to keep it. Buy it yourself if self-employed. Work long enough to qualify for your company's retiree health-care coverage until Medicare begins.

A recent AARP study found that more people age fifty to sixty-four are uninsured today than in the past.[1] The high cost of health insurance is causing many to go uninsured, but the cost of health care may be even higher than the cost of premiums.

Companies are cutting back on the medical benefits provided to retirees. Watson Wyatt Worldwide, a human resources consulting firm that works with employers, released a study that found large employers now typically pay more than half of total retiree medical expenses. This is down sharply from the late 1980s. Increasing health care costs are forcing companies to scale back how much they are willing to offer.

Sylvester J. Schieber, an author of the study, says, "The burden on future retirees to pay for their own medical costs is increasing dramatically, and far too few employees are prepared for these looming changes." By 2031, companies are expected to pay less than 10 percent of total medical expenses for retirees.[2]

It is rare for someone to have enough resources to self-insure for health care. Only if you have several million in cash assets should you even try to get by without health insurance.

I (Larry) was in perfect health until I was fifty. It seems, however, that I had only a fifty-year guarantee on my body. After that it has just worn out. Having health insurance has allowed me to receive care and still have something left to live on—something left for my wife, Judy, to live on if I die first, something left for my children and grandchildren, something left for ministries.

For me (Ron), on the other hand, I am thankful to be in good health. When I turned sixty, I jumped out of an airplane (skydiving) just to prove I could do it and that I wasn't so old after all. Although the cost of health insurance is expensive, I would not think of dropping it, even with my good health.

How much health insurance can you afford? What if you can't afford the amount of insurance you need? The answer is simple: Get all the insurance you can for the money you have available. A health insurance policy with a high deductible, such as $5,000, can provide catastrophic coverage. These premiums are much more affordable and limit your financial risk from major illnesses.

Life insurance. It helps to answer four questions when making a decision about life insurance. Let's consider them one at a time.

Why buy life insurance? You want this insurance for two main reasons: (1) to protect your family income if the breadwinner dies and (2) to protect your estate so that it can be passed on to your heirs. In return for your paying a premium, the insurance company assumes the risk of loss of income or erosion of the estate through taxes.

During the times of biblical history, a man's sons took over his farm or business and provided for the family. If he had no son, his closest male heir assumed that responsibility. Today life insurance is a substitute means of providing for his family if a man dies prematurely.

How much life insurance do you need? Through financial media, many financial planners quote a general rule of obtaining insurance equal to ten times your current income. While this may work well for a young family, you can use a more specific approach. The amount of life insurance you need depends upon your debt, the income sources your survivors will have, your age and the age of your survivors, the amount of assets you have, and other factors.

You can find some assistance in answering this question by completing the Life Insurance Needs Analysis chart on the following page. After you complete it, review it with your spouse. Make sure that your spouse is comfortable with the amount of insurance you are considering.

LIFE INSURANCE NEEDS ANALYSIS

1. **Annual** living expenses of survivors (spouse, children, etc.)
(consider 70% of current family living expenses) $ _____ (1)

2. Expected **annual** benefits/income to your survivors:
   a. Social Security benefits $ _____
   b. Survivor's pension benefits $ _____
   c. Survivor's earned income $ _____
   d. Other income $ _____
   Total expected annual benefits/income $ _____ (2)

3. Net living expense shortage (or surplus)
(Line 1 minus line 2) $ _____ (3)

4. Amount of capital required to produce living
expenses shortage $ _____ (4)
(Line 3 divided by projected rate of return of
invested capital. Consider using a conservative
rate of return to adjust for inflation.)
Inflation-adjusted rate of return _____%

5. Plus other lump-sum expenses
   a. Final expenses/estate costs $ _____
   b. Mortgage payoff $ _____
   c. Payoff of other debts $ _____
   d. Education fund or other $ _____
   e. Emergency fund $ _____
   Total lump-sum expenses $ _____ (5)

6. Total assets required (Line 4 plus line 5) $ _____ (6)

7. Present assets
   a. Income-producing assets $ _____
   b. Present life insurance $ _____
   Total present available assets $ _____ (7)

8. Amount of life insurance to be added, if any
(Line 6 minus line 7) $ _____ (8)

This worksheet is only designed to provide an estimate of life insurance needs.
Two families with identical numbers may reasonably conclude that their insurance needs differ significantly.

How long do you need life insurance? When you were younger and in the accumulation stage of life with a growing family, you had a need for significant life insurance. However, this period of peak insurance ends as children become self-sufficient adults.

As you grow older and have fewer dependents, your need for life insurance lessens. Updating and completing the Life Insurance Needs Analysis chart is helpful to determine if you still need life insurance. You may still need to have insurance available when you're in your sixties or seventies to pay any estate taxes due on a nonliquid estate. Second, life insurance provides instant liquidity and the benefits are tax-free. Money may be needed to pay funeral and burial expenses without cashing in a CD or selling mutual funds. Having some life insurance available may provide more time for your spouse or estate to sell a business or other assets at more opportune times.

And make sure your family has a written plan concerning the use of the insurance, along with alternatives for additional help when you die (i.e., employment of surviving spouse, family help, sources of counsel, etc.).

What is the best kind of life insurance? There is no "best" kind of insurance. That's a little like walking into a doctor's office and asking, "What's your best operation?" The type of life insurance that's best for your family depends on your specific needs. Although life insurance comes in hundreds of wrappers, there are basically two types of insurance available: term and whole- (or permanent) life.

1. Term. Term insurance means insurance that is purchased for a specific period of time. This product provides the maximum coverage for the lowest initial premiums. Generally, term insurance is better for young couples with limited incomes because of its low cost and because families need maximum coverage when their children are young.

We recommend buying term for the periods of maximum need. Buy for terms where the premium is guaranteed, such as twenty-year guaranteed level premium. As you enter your fifties and sixties, you may save money at restaurants with a senior citizen discount, but buying a new term policy will be expensive.

2. Whole- or permanent life. Whole life means that the policy is in force for your whole life. Whole life also is known as cash-value insurance because it accumulates a cash reserve. Variable life, hybrid (whole-life combined with term), and universal life are derivatives of permanent life.

The premiums for whole-life are more expensive at first than a term policy. In a sense, the insurance buyer overpays in the early years so that he or she can underpay in later years. This feature is what creates a cash value in the policy; it is a type of forced savings.

Yet, while many people say forced savings is unnecessary, our experience has been that most people do a poor job of saving. So this aspect of a whole life policy may or may not be helpful, depending on your discipline to save. Although the policy contract may require premiums to be paid for your lifetime, the policy can be paid up much sooner if you reinvest the dividends back into the policy. The primary disadvantage of a whole-life policy is that the premiums are relatively high in the early years, especially when compared to the coverage provided.

No single plan fits everyone. For long-term needs, we recommend going with a strong insurance company and a good agent who will be around to service you ten or twenty years down the road. The product you choose will depend on how much cash you have, but the traditional whole-life policies may be the best choice for your base level of coverage. Use term insurance for additional coverage for children, certain large debts, or other defined periods of time.

Disability insurance—insuring your paycheck. How dependent is your family on earned income? If they're like most of us, they're very dependent on it. And statistics reveal that you have one chance in three of suffering a long-term disability sometime between the ages of thirty-five and sixty-five. Even so, disability income protection is often overlooked in financial planning.

If available, the most economical place to obtain disability insurance is with a group plan through your employer. Most importantly, obtain long-term disability coverage. It often starts after six months or perhaps one year. Consider short-term disability only if very inexpensively available through your employer. Use your emergency savings to cover the first few months of a disability.

If you are self-employed or your employer does not provide group disability insurance, you can buy an individual policy. This is what Bill wished he had done. Or, more accurately, this is what Bill's family wished he had done.

Bill, a fifty-two-year-old successful owner of a home building company, had a skiing accident and hit his head on a tree. After six weeks of unconsciousness, he awoke but had lost much of his memory and cognitive ability.

After six months of therapy, he returned home with most of his physical abilities, but his mind was not the same. His math skill of estimating jobs, his short-term memory, and his ability to concentrate and read contracts were mostly gone. His business continued for a while as his crews finished existing jobs, but gradually his business (his source of income) dried up despite the best efforts of his family to keep it going.

If Bill had died in that accident, his adequate life insurance would have provided for his family. He had health insurance to pay the $100,000 medical bill from hospital, therapy, and prescription drug costs. But he had no disability insurance. He had nothing to replace his paycheck. He was employable in some jobs, but not his former job, so Social Security would not pay any disability benefits.

How much disability coverage do you need? And what kind of policy should you obtain? Most insurers won't allow the amount of disability coverage to exceed approximately 60 percent of your earned income. (This is to reduce any incentives to fake disabilities.)

Perhaps the single most important question in evaluating disability income coverage is the insurer's definition of disability: Is it the inability to perform the main duties of *your occupation* or *any occupation,* or does it relate to some *loss of earnings* that you experience? Know this answer before purchasing. Also, be sure your agent explains the length of the benefit period, the waiting period, the cost-of-living riders, and the treatment of partial disabilities.

While many people overlook disability insurance, even more overlook another type of insurance. As you begin to approach your late fifties and sixties, consider the next form of insurance we recommend: long-term care insurance.

Long-term care insurance. Before you skip to the next section, because you would rather not think about a possible nursing-home stay, let us suggest you consider a few facts. We call these the Seven Realities of Long-Term Care.

1. Long-term care includes a broad range of services provided in any setting outside a hospital. It includes home-health care, respite care, adult day care, care in a nursing home, personal or custodial care in the home, and care in an assisted-living facility.

2. Of Americans over sixty-five, 60 percent will need some long-term care during their lifetime.[3]

3. Neither Medicare nor Medicare supplemental insurance policies were designed to pay long-term care. They are for acute care and post-hospital stays for short-term rehabilitation.

4. Medicaid will only pay for long-term care for the poor, usually defined as having $2,000 or less in assets.

5. The national average for one year of nursing home care is $50,000 per year.[4]

6. The average nursing home stay is two and a half years. One out of ten will stay there five years or longer.[5]

7. The annual costs for long-term care are rising and may triple in the next twenty years.[6]

Given these realities, how will you pay for long-term care? There are basically four choices.

- Self-insure. You could pay for the care from your assets. The drawback to this approach is that the significant cost of care could wipe out a lifetime of saving.

- Use Medicaid. If you spend all you have, then Medicaid will pay for your nursing home coverage. Few, if any, middle-class Americans will qualify for Medicaid initially.

- Rely upon family members. As we discussed in chapter 7, families have some responsibility to provide care for aging parents. You must ask yourself if they will have the time and expertise to care for you. Most parents prefer independence. Geographical or emotional distance, financial limitations, and physical space requirements may make this approach difficult.

- Obtain long-term care insurance. This option will provide coverage for nursing home stays, home health care, assisted living, and/or other types of care. It will preserve your assets by paying the costs of your care. Of course, this insurance is not free.

How much does long-term care insurance cost? Well, it depends. The variable factors are your age when obtaining the insurance initially, your health, and the benefits you select. Let's assume that Lee, age sixty, and his wife, Carol, age fifty-nine, are healthy nonsmokers. Here is what they can expect to pay and the related benefits.

Sample Long-Term Insurance Premiums

Lee	$151.65 per month[7]
Carol	143.28 per month
Total	$294.93 per month

Specific information for the above policy:

- $120 per day for nursing home care
- $120 per day for home health care
- Lifetime benefits (will pay for care as long as needed until death)
- Inflation rider of 5 percent per year (benefit will be $126 in year two, and increase $6 per year)
- Elimination period of ninety days (like a deductible, no coverage during first ninety days)

Most policies begin coverage either when you show mental impairment, such as Alzheimer's disease, or when you can no longer perform by yourself any two of the six activities of daily living. These activities include bathing, eating, dressing, toileting, continence, and walking/transferring.

Many people spend a lifetime saving and doing all the right things in planning for retirement and older age. But then they neglect to address the potential risk to their financial wealth that long-term care costs pose. If you have some assets and income, then you are a suitable candidate for long-term care insurance.

You, as a member of the "sandwich generation," face a pivotal role in your extended family. As we discussed in chapter 7, you may be or may already have been responsible for caring for elderly parents and assisting in long-term care issues. You may have realized that you wish to obtain long-term care insurance for yourself so you can maintain your independence and not burden your children and grandchildren.

At times the insurance industry has used fear and emotional appeals to induce people into buying their product. Some have done this with long-term care insurance. The National Association of Insurance Commissioners, an organization of all the state insurance commissioners, tried to clarify who should consider long-term care insurance with the following consumer information.

Is Long-Term Care Insurance Right for You?

(Source: *A Shopper's Guide to Long-Term Care Insurance,*
by the National Association of Insurance Commissioners)

You should NOT buy long-term care insurance if:

• You can't afford the premiums.
• You have limited assets.
• Your only source of income is a Social Security benefit or Supplemental Security Income (SSI).
• You often have trouble paying for utilities, food, medicine, or other important needs.

You should CONSIDER buying long-term care insurance if:

• You have significant assets and income.
• You want to protect some of your assets and income.
• You want to pay for your own care.
• You want to stay independent of the support of others.

Liability insurance. The final type of insurance you likely need is protection from liability. This liability may arise from accidents on your property (home), accidents with your property (auto), or accidents from other actions.

- Ray, excitedly talking on a cell phone, runs a red light and hits a van carrying preschool children. Does he have enough liability coverage on his auto insurance?

- The Andrews love to have their grandchildren play in their pool. Their grandchildren invite some friends over. One of the friends, whose father is a trial lawyer, dives in shallow water and incurs a paralyzing spinal cord injury. Do the Andrews have enough liability coverage on their home policy?

- Patty hooks her golf swing wildly to the left. The golf ball bounces into the highway and causes an accident. Does she have an "umbrella" liability policy?

While the probability of these examples happening to you may seem unlikely, they are not far-fetched. Accidents can and do happen. Too often, people focus on insuring property—cars, boat, and house—and neglect insuring the liability. The common ways to obtain liability coverage are through home insurance, auto insurance, an "umbrella" liability coverage for general actions or negligence, and professional liability for self-employed professionals. Because of our litigious society, liability coverage is important to protect your assets and preserve your estate.

It is confusing what actions or negligence various policies cover. Your agent can help you understand the differences. For example, if a visiting child has an accident in your home or on your property, then your home-owner's liability policy protects you. But if you provide day-care services from your home for money, then you have a business. Most home-owner policies will not provide liability protection for a business, even a hobby or part-time business.

Let's look at landowner John Doe. He lets friends hunt on his land for free, and he will have liability coverage through his home or farm policy. But if he charges them to hunt and they sue for damages from an accident, then most home or farm policies will not provide coverage. John Doe, landowner, should have a business rider or policy. Your local agent earns his keep by helping you understand the ins and outs of liability coverage.

Obtain liability coverage, say through an umbrella policy, that approximates your net worth. Remember our theme throughout this chapter: cover the catastrophic, even if it is unlikely (like the example of the pool accident). Consider self-insuring the likely but not catastrophic, like a deer causing $300 of car damage.

A FINAL INSURANCE THOUGHT

Remember one of the best forms of insurance: take care of yourself. Eat healthy, exercise regularly, rest plentifully, avoid stress diligently, and get health-care checkups faithfully. You can spend small fortunes on health insurance, disability insurance, and life insurance but sometimes overlook the practically free protection of taking care of the *"temple of the Holy Spirit"* (2 Corinthians 6:16).

Yet even the health-food nut who runs six miles a day will someday cross life's finish line into death. The next two chapters help you get ready for finishing well.

ASK LARRY

Q. I was recently laid off when my employer closed one of their plants. What are my options for health insurance now that I've lost my job? I won't have any insurance when I leave this company.

A. Under the COBRA Act, you can continue the insurance that your company offers (if they have twenty or more employees) for up to eighteen months. However, you probably will pay the total cost of the insurance—the employee's portion *and* the company's portion, plus a small administrative fee. In general, you will pay 103 percent of the total cost.

I would recommend the COBRA provision only if you have a pre-existing condition that precludes you from getting insurance elsewhere. Usually, the coverage in a company's group plan is better than what you can buy on your own, but most people don't need that kind of coverage. More commonly, what you need is a higher-deductible disaster insurance—in other words, a major medical insurance plan with a deductible of $500 to $1,000.

Additionally, some states have state insurance health plans for those who have been turned down for health insurance for whatever reason. However, these plans are expensive and/or may be available only to lower-income individuals. Unfortunately, the bottom line is that there are no real bargains in health insurance these days.

ASK RON

Q. When do I no longer need life insurance?

A. When your assets can pay your obligations and support any dependents, then you no longer need life insurance. (In other words, when your productive assets reach the point of generating enough income to provide for your survivors.). Until that time, life insurance is an umbrella of protection that provides the resources needed if you die before meeting your financial goals.

Retirement may be such a time when you no longer need life insurance. At retirement, your income should be set (Social Security, pension plans, annuities, and investments). Your debts should be paid off and your children self-sufficient. If your spouse's needs would also be met after the death of the provider, then there would not be a need for insurance to supply additional provision. An additional consideration for keeping some insurance is if your estate needs liquidity or to pay estate taxes.

ASK LARRY

Q. My widowed mother is concerned that all her money is going to go to a nursing home someday. She is seventy-five years old and wants to sign all her assets over to us. But she still wants to have control of the assets. We are unsure about this and are considering long-term care insurance for her. Is this insurance a good idea for us?

A. Many people have tried to appear poor on paper by transferring assets to family members and then trying to qualify for Medicaid to pay for nursing home costs. I have thought the practice to be dishonest. The states have wised up to your mother's plans now. Generally, assets must be given away or transferred at least three years before eligibility for Medicaid.

Your decision about long-term care insurance is truly a matter of protecting assets. Let's say, for instance, that your mother had $500,000 worth of assets. Let's further assume she decided to self-insure rather than obtain long-term care insurance. If her nursing home costs $50,000 per year and she spent four years there, then her assets would be reduced to $300,000. The state would not pay for her stay because she had available assets. The most your mother could pay for would be ten years.

On the other hand, let's say she had to pay $5,000 per year for a policy because of her age. Let's say she paid the policy for five years and then entered a nursing home for four years. After that four years, her assets would be $475,000 [$500,000 - ($5,000 x 5)] instead of $300,000 above.

Long-term care insurance is expensive because the cost of nursing home care is expensive. However, it is generally appropriate for those with larger amounts of assets (about $250,000 or more).

Let's assume that a single seventy-five-year-old individual owned a home, a car, and a savings account of about $100,000. That person's nursing home stay would consume all those assets in approximately two years. Medicaid would then pick up the costs for as long as he or she would require. In this example, it's really a toss-up whether long-term care insurance is a good deal for them. Long-term care insurance premiums could eat up much of their savings account.

Ask Ron

Q. My parents, who are in their seventies, need a health-care supplement. They both have Medicare but no supplemental policy. Do you recommend supplemental insurance for Medicare?

A. Yes, Medicare covers the major items but not everything. There is a substantial difference between what medical care costs and what Medicare will pay. I recommend that you purchase a supplemental insurance policy. The nonpaid portion of medical health care can put a great strain on your parents' finances. In my estimation, supplemental insurance is wise for the majority of Medicare recipients.

Ask Yourself

- Overall, am I using insurance as a wise financial planning tool or as something to trust in?
- Have I reviewed all my insurance policies and their appropriateness? What types of insurance do I currently have that I probably do not need?
- Do I have adequate life insurance? If I think so, would my spouse or other heirs agree?
- Are my choices of beneficiaries consistent with my current estate plans?
- Do my spouse and other heirs know what insurance policies I have? Do they know the location of the policies?

finances to her. She remembered her usual response: "Hon, you are good at all that. I trust you, and whatever you do is fine with me."

As long as she knew the ATM password and had enough checks to write, she was more interested in her household responsibilities and maintaining their relationships with friends and family. Besides, it seemed that Bob took some pride in the fact that his management of their financial affairs allowed his wife not to have to worry about money.

Bob had often called her the social coordinator for the family. She had playfully teased him about being the financial nerd for the family. Now she wished she had taken some cross-training and that Bob had left a better trail to follow.

We, like most financial and investment counselors, have met with many new widows like Linda. All too often they carry financial burdens and anxiety hand-in-hand with their grief. Unfortunately, it is less frequently that we hear of a widow who has financial confidence because she knew her family's financial matters, the location of important assets and documents, key advisers, and the plan for the future. We desire that your family be of the latter type.

Certainly, men can end up as widowers and be in the dark about the family finances. Many women take on more of the financial knowledge and responsibility in their families because their skills and gifts equip them to do it well. So our recommendations can apply equally to the widower as well.

But the more common outcome is that the man dies first. The most recent U.S. Census found that 45 percent of women aged sixty-five and older were widowed, while only 14 percent of men at that age were widowed. Seventy-four percent of men aged sixty-five and older are married, while only 43 percent of women are still married.[1] A casual observation of the greater numbers of elderly women in churches or nursing homes confirms these statistics. Husbands and wives need to acknowledge this likelihood that the husband will die first and to plan for it.

We understand that talking and planning about our demise is neither easy nor pleasant. Certainly it is not a weekly dinner conversation topic. If you know Jesus as your personal Savior, then you will be enjoying heaven. You will be fine; we are not worried about you. But what about your loved ones left behind after your departure?

Do you recall the romantic opening line of Elizabeth Barrett Browning's famous poem? "How do I love thee? Let me count the ways." Well, one way to count your love is to prepare a trail, a road map, really a final letter. Consider it your last love letter. This better be good because your will, a listing of your assets, and other final documents are your last words. The absence of your "last love letter" can generate fear, frustration, worry, and doubt.

Make it your goal for your spouse to realize your love after you are gone. May your spouse know that your love was like that of the last line of Mrs. Browning's poem: "I shall but love thee better after death."

A LOVE LETTER TO LAST

Without delay we urge you to write your love letter and organize your estate. Crown Financial Ministry, the organization for which I (Larry) serve as chairman of the board, has an excellent resource for leaving a "love letter" trail for your wife. Titled *Set Your House in Order,* this workbook provides fill-in-the-blank forms for you to complete all the necessary information for your estate, funeral plans, location of key documents, and so on. To obtain a copy, call Crown toll free at 888-972-7696 or visit the web site at www.crown.org. Completion of this workbook will provide your spouse with all that he or she needs.

If you don't buy the workbook or you wish to begin now, we want you to start your love letter by completing the worksheet on the following pages.

ORGANIZING YOUR ESTATE

Date: _____

WILL AND/OR TRUST

The Will (Trust) is located: _____
The person designated to carry out its provisions is: _____
If that person cannot or will not serve, the alternate is: _____
Lawyer: _____ Phone: _____
Accountant: _____ Phone: _____

FINANCIAL BENEFITS

1. Company Benefits
My/our heirs will begin receiving company benefits as follows: _____
_____
Contact: _____ Phone: _____

2. Banking Information
Bank: _____
Type of Account (Checking, Savings, CD, etc.) _____
Account Number or CD Number _____
Safe Deposit Box Information _____

Bank: _____
Type of Account (Checking, Savings, CD, etc.) _____
Account Number or CD Number _____

Bank: _____
Type of Account (Checking, Savings, CD, etc.) _____
Account Number or CD Number _____

3. Veteran's Benefits
You are/are not eligible for veteran's benefits: _____
To receive these benefits you should do the following: _____

4. Life Insurance Coverage
Insurance Company: _____ Policy #_____
Face Value: _____ Person Insured: _____ Beneficiary: _____

Insurance Company: _____ Policy #_____
Face Value: _____ Person Insured: _____ Beneficiary: _____

Insurance Company: _____ Policy #_____
Face Value: _____ Person Insured: _____ Beneficiary: _____

INVESTMENTS

Description: _____ Account #: _____
Beneficiary [for IRAs, 401(k), annuities] _____
Contact: _____

Description: _____ Account #: _____
Beneficiary, if applicable _____
Contact: _____

Description: _____ Account #: _____
Beneficiary, if applicable _____
Contact: _____

Description: _____ Account #: _____
Beneficiary, if applicable _____
Contact: _____

MILITARY SERVICE HISTORY

Branch of Service: _____ Service Number: _____
Length of Service: _____ From: _____ Until: _____
Rank: _____ Location and description of important military
documents: _____

FUNERAL INSTRUCTIONS

Funeral Home: _____
Address: _____ Phone: _____
My/our place of burial is located at: _____
Request burial in the following manner: _____
Request that memorial gifts be given to the following church/organizations:
Name: _____ Address: _____
Name: _____ Address: _____

In addition to documenting assets and leaving a love letter, husbands may consider providing "on-the-job training." Husbands, let your wives actually manage the home finances for at least the next year. This would include opening the mail of investment accounts, meeting with advisers, reviewing insurance, paying bills, balancing checkbooks, maintaining the budget, and negotiating major purchases. Certainly, many women currently handle some or all of these chores. Although some women may resist taking on more responsibility, both husbands and wives should see it as necessary cross-training. How much easier for a wife to undertake these financial responsibilities now, with assistance from her husband, than later all alone.

Remember that you are trying to make the practical aspects of living life after the death of a spouse easier for those left behind. Other information, in addition to the worksheet provided on the previous pages, to consider preparing for your spouse includes the following:

- Location of important documents, such as deeds, birth certificates, car titles, wills, power of attorney, and living will
- Preferred ministers for funeral
- Key advisers and phone numbers, such as attorney, accountant, investment adviser, insurance agent, banker
- List of debts owed
- Computer programs (and any passwords) containing important information
- List of property loaned out to others
- Location of insurance policies, such as life insurance
- Description and location of any valuable personal property, such as coin collection or antiques
- Location of current-year tax information (someone still has to file an income tax return for the year in which you died) and past year returns

- Location of any hidden cash or "buried treasures"
- Keys and locks—any safe combinations, location of safe deposit keys, extra keys hidden for house or car, keys for padlocks

WHAT FINANCIAL DECISIONS SHOULD A WIDOW MAKE AFTER THE DEATH OF HER HUSBAND?

None for a while. Simply grieve and wait. After the death of a spouse, no significant financial decision should be made during the grieving process. We recommend waiting a year before making any significant decisions, such as selling a house or making major portfolio changes.

The knee-jerk reaction is to act quickly because the memories and grief are painful. Jan thought she couldn't bear to remain in their house with five acres in the country after Jim died. So her daughter convinced her to sell the homeplace in a small Kentucky town and move closer to her in a Chicago suburb. After a few years Jan longed to be back near her friends, her church, her town, and, yes, her old house.

Another widow, Barbara, met with her insurance agent three weeks after the death of her husband. Fortunately, her husband had enough life insurance to meet her needs. The insurance agent delivered the check promptly and courteously. He then offered Barbara an investment that paid an attractive rate of interest but would require a five-year commitment. Barbara accepted.

In the next few years Barbara had several occasions where she needed a portion of that money—to help a son during an emergency, to buy an adjoining lot to her residence, and to help fund a business she wished to start. But she realized she had acted too quickly in locking up the insurance money.

Other important activities after the death of a spouse include the following:

1. Locate all life insurance policies, including any life benefits that may be part of your health insurance policy and any credit life benefits on any outstanding loans. Call the local agent or write to each company and request a claim form and information on any requirements needed to process the claim. For instance, you will need to enclose a certified copy of the death certificate when you submit the completed claim forms. The insurance company will tell you what other things you need to know when you file a claim.

2. Contact your local Social Security office. You likely will be entitled to receive a survivor's benefit, that is a portion of your spouse's Social Security benefit. Also, the estate of each deceased person, whether he or she had begun Social Security or not, is eligible for a small death benefit. The Social Security personnel can give you information over the phone or provide a pamphlet that explains your benefits and the requirements for filing a claim to receive benefits for you and/or any children under age eighteen.

3. If the spouse was a veteran, contact the Veterans Administration for information on any benefits that are available to a surviving spouse and dependent children of veterans.

4. Titles to properties owned jointly with rights of survivorship will need to be converted to the ownership of the survivor. The change of title will require a certified copy of the death certificate. These properties might include the titles on autos, houses, or investment accounts.

5. Contact the spouse's current or any former employers' human resources departments to determine the eligibility for any pension, life insurance, or other retirement plan information.

6. Be sure to check with the bank to find out what you need to do about checking and savings accounts. Notify any credit card companies to have the name of the deceased person removed from the account. Some companies require a certified copy of the death certificate.

As God said early in the Bible, *"For this reason a man shall leave his father and his mother, and be joined to his wife; and they shall become one flesh"* (Genesis 2:24). The translation of this verse, actually the application of it, means if you are "one flesh" or one person, then you have to be communicating. This communication applies to financial and provisional matters in addition to romantic and relational matters.

Communication is not easy, though, and may be misinterpreted. Consider the case of the Illinois man who left the snow-filled streets of Chicago for a vacation in Florida. His wife was on a business trip and was planning to meet him there the next day.

When he reached his hotel, he decided to send his wife a quick e-mail. Unfortunately, when typing her address, he missed one letter, and his note was directed instead to an elderly woman whose husband had passed away only the day before.

When the grieving widow checked her e-mail, she took one look at the monitor, let out a piercing scream, and fell to the floor in a faint.

At the sound of her hitting the floor, her family rushed into the room and saw this note on the screen:

"Dearest Wife,

Just got checked in. Everything prepared for your arrival tomorrow.

Love,

Your Husband

P.S. Sure is hot down here."

ASK LARRY

Q. Is it a good idea to leave money to my wife in a trust, so she can spend the income but not the principal during her lifetime? I'm concerned that if I die, somebody, even a future husband, might come along and trick her out of our insurance money and other assets.

A. There's nothing wrong with leaving assets in trust for your spouse. In many instances, if the person doesn't really want to be bothered with the management of the money, it's a good financial planning tool.

However, I must caution you about something. If you're committing these assets (including the income) to be used only for your widow, in my opinion, that is unscriptural. If your wife remarries, she is bound to her new husband, and they are to be one. And whatever assets she has available should also be available to him.

I understand the argument against that very well: What if she marries a scoundrel? Well, you have to trust her judgment, and she has to be smart enough not to marry a scoundrel. Once married, they are to be one person, with no barrier between them. If you leave this money only to her, and her future husband has no access to it, even for living expenses, you have created an artificial barrier between them.

The apostle Paul said, *"Wives, be subject to your own husbands, as to the Lord"* (Ephesians 5:22). As a Christian, you don't want to be guilty of interfering in a future relationship. So you need to discuss this with your wife and have a clear understanding. Ultimately, if you do leave it in trust, make the trust flexible enough that she and her future husband can have access to the funds according to how they feel led.

I know that my counsel runs contrary to most of the advice today. But the world's advice is based primarily on what the world says, not on what God's Word says.

Q. In light of your cancer, what financial discussions have you had with your wife?

A. Something I had always done, even before my cancer diagnosis, was prepare a brief written plan for Judy. Every two years or so, I would write down for her what I would do. I would list various accounts and key advisers for her. We would also review where important documents were located and go over our will and estate plans.

After my illness I began using a CPA for our taxes so that Judy could have a person to go to who already knew our situation and could help her. For investments I use a financial adviser who knows me, knows our plans, and knows my wife. So I have tried to make a transition easier for her if I go to be with Lord first.

Q. I have been widowed for several years. I have been dating a single man who is divorced. He has been successful in business and wants me to sign a prenuptial agreement. He says he wants to protect our children from other marriages, but I am uneasy about it. What does the Bible say about pre-nuptial or premarital agreements?

A. In my opinion there can be no premarital agreements except those established in God's Word. Ephesians 5:22 and 25 says, *"Wives, be subject to your own husbands, as to the Lord. . . . Husbands, love your wives, just as Christ also loved the church and gave Himself up for her."* Genesis 2:24 says, *"A man shall leave his father and his mother, and shall cleave to his wife; and they shall become one flesh."*

In other words, they are to be one. It makes no difference if either of them has been married before because when they marry they have only one spouse. Whatever she has belongs to him; whatever he has belongs to her. If they are to be one, there can be no barrier between them. A Christian who approaches marriage with any other attitude presupposes that the marriage will not survive, since a premarital agreement is a plan for dissolution.

God's Word tells us to yield our rights to Him and to one another. Many good marriages have been destroyed through a lack of faith and a lack of trust, and a premarital agreement would, with rare exception, take all the faith and trust out of the marriage.

In your estate planning you two may be able to specify that remaining assets are to be distributed to your respective children and grandchildren. For example, if you married and he died before you, then those assets could be placed in a trust. The resulting income from those assets could support you during your life. Upon your death the assets could be distributed to his children, not yours.

ASK RON

Q. I'm a widow in my mid-sixties. Should I pay off my home or invest the money my husband left me?

A. Although I don't know your specific risk tolerance, my experience is that a widow of your age is very conservative, as you likely should be. Anything can happen in our economy, and any investment can be lost. Regardless of what happens in the economy, a mortgage liability will survive because the lenders are protected by law. Take a portion of your assets to pay off and retire your home mortgage. Keep some funds available and liquid.

Many people never thought they would lose a large portion of their wealth, but they did when the economy turned down. Any investment, whether it is stocks, a farm, oil and gas, precious metals, art, or anything else, can decrease when the economy sours.

Do what the Bible says, *"Listen to counsel and accept discipline, that you may be wise the rest of your days. Many are the plans are in a man's heart, but the counsel of the LORD will stand"* (Proverbs 19:20–21). In other words, take your counsel from the Lord. He is your primary counselor. If you have peace about paying off your home, do it. If you don't have peace about paying it off, don't do it.

But if you plan on staying in the house, my counsel to my own wife would be to pay off the mortgage.

Q. Your entire career has consisted of helping people reach their financial goals. How do you do it within your own family? What financial discussions have you had with your wife?

A. I remember talking with Judy (Larry and I are close, but we do not have the same wife; they just have the same name!) about some of our estate plans. She told me, "I don't need to understand all the technical stuff and legalese. I just need to know whom to call, and I do."

If I go on to be with our Lord first, she knows she can depend on our financial adviser. He is a partner in our firm who acts as our personal financial adviser. Judy knows he will provide her with wise counsel and security for our family.

Because a marriage is a team, we talk and set goals together. Certainly, I have more of the professional background to implement our goals, but we set them together. Over the years we have taken a getaway weekend (we call them "mini-summits") to set goals in our marriage, finances, parenting, spiritual growth, and physical areas.

We get away from the distractions to enjoy each other and have some recreation and romance. During these times Judy and I have talked about our financial goals and details. She knows what we own, what life insurance we have, what investments we have. She doesn't particularly like the financial matters, but she is aware of what we have and where to look for them.

In addition, I have used money management software to organize our finances for Judy. Some of my children are skilled enough on the computer to help her if she has any difficulty understanding the software.

ASK YOURSELF

- If I died today, how much difficulty would my spouse have in handling our financial and legal matters?

- How would my spouse answer the above question? (Why not ask your spouse?)

- What excuses have I been using not to complete my "last love letter" to my family?

- If my spouse and I were killed in an accident together, would anyone else know how to proceed with the handling of our estate? Who else should at least know the whereabouts of my last love letter?

- Does my will need to be updated?

- Will my spouse want, or be able to afford, to stay where we are living now if I died?

We have seen bumper stickers expressing similar sentiments, like the one frequently seen on motor homes: "We're spending our kids' inheritance."

There's an assumption underlying these statements. It is that you can know exactly when and under what circumstances you will die. If that were the case, you could plan to have the last penny spent just at the moment of death. Or perhaps have your check to the undertaker bounce. Unfortunately, the most frequent comment you hear after someone has died is, "Poor John didn't plan on dying so soon." People forget, or ignore, that *"it is appointed for men to die once and after this comes judgment"* (Hebrews 9:27). Everyone will die, yet few plan on dying so soon.

PLANNING FOR THE INEVITABLE

Our perspective on estate planning, therefore, must be based on true realities. We don't know the details of your estate, but we do know the following true realities apply to you and to us.

We all will die.

We will take nothing with us.

We will probably die at a time other than when we would like.

These realities create a number of practical challenges, the most significant of which is described in Romans 6:23: *"For the wages of sin is death, but the free gift of God is eternal life in Christ Jesus our Lord."* One who dies without having accepted the gift of Jesus Christ as payment for personal sin is eternally separated from God.

Financial challenges do not exist in eternity. Our prayer is that if you have never accepted the free gift of God's Son as payment for your sins, you would do so and take the most important estate-planning decision you can ever take. A simple prayer, similar to the following one, lays the foundation for your estate in eternity: "Father, I acknowledge my separation from You, and based on the death of the Lord Jesus Christ as payment for my sins, I accept Your free gift of salvation. Thank You for saving me and making me heir to the greatest estate—heaven."

The second challenge with death is planning. While we eagerly enjoy planning for fun events, such as vacations and parties, we don't enjoy planning for events surrounding death. Because we don't like unpleasant chores, we often procrastinate.

Unless you plan the distribution of your earthly estate, the government will distribute it for you. Your spouse, relatives, or friends are not allowed to plan for that distribution. Only the owner of assets can plan for their distribution through a will. The government may not have the same objectives for your estate that you do.

Additionally, if proper planning has not been done, final expenses can siphon off as much as 70 percent of an estate. These expenses are for probating the will, federal estate taxes, state inheritance taxes, attorney's fees, accountant's fees, funeral expenses, and the like.

Another financial challenge resulting from poor planning is an estate that lacks enough liquidity (that is, available cash) to meet final expenses. While there may be more than enough total assets to cover these expenses, those assets (such as farmland or interest in a business) are not readily accessible. Therefore, assets must be sold, often at depressed values, just to generate the cash needed to pay the estate's expenses.

Our theme throughout this book has been making your wealth last. You probably assumed we meant trying to make your wealth last until the end of your life or until the end of your spouse's life. But our ultimate goal is to help you make your wealth last beyond your life, a legacy to continue past you.

If your wealth does last beyond your lifetime, then you will have to transfer your wealth. I (Ron) have developed the following flowchart describing the wealth transfer decision-making process. You also could think of it as a legacy-transfer process. We will touch only on the key concepts of this process in this chapter. I have written an entire book on wealth transfer called *Splitting Heirs,* due to release soon. It describes in detail this process, the ten important wealth-transfer principles, and their biblical basis. We recommend you make your wealth transfer decisions in the order of the decisions presented on the following chart.

WEALTH-TRANSFER DECISION-MAKING PROCESS

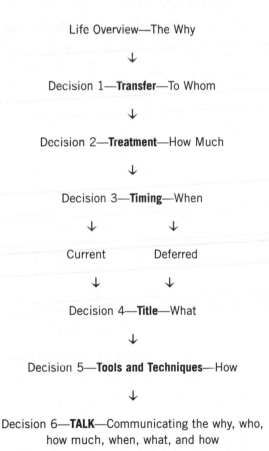

Life Overview—The Why

↓

Decision 1—**Transfer**—To Whom

↓

Decision 2—**Treatment**—How Much

↓

Decision 3—**Timing**—When

↓   ↓

Current   Deferred

↓   ↓

Decision 4—**Title**—What

↓

Decision 5—**Tools and Techniques**—How

↓

Decision 6—**TALK**—Communicating the why, who,
how much, when, what, and how

LIFE OVERVIEW—IN A NUTSHELL

The starting point of this flowchart is the big picture. Think of your life overview as how you live out biblical stewardship and follow God's design for your life. Biblical stewardship is the accomplishment of God-given objectives, using God-given resources. Let's begin to implement the decisions with your life overview in mind. Your spiritual gifts and interests may lead you to transfer your wealth very differently than your neighbors.

Decision 1: Transfer—Who gets your wealth? Because we all entered this world with nothing and will leave with nothing (Job 1:21), someone else will end up with your wealth.

At a funeral of a fellow millionaire, one man asked a mutual friend, "How much did he leave?"

The friend wisely replied, "All of it."

Three choices exist for who will end up with your wealth.

1. *Your heirs.* These are individuals you choose, usually your family. This is the most popular choice of Americans.
2. *Charity.* This is the most tax-effective choice.
3. *Government.* Taxes to the federal government and/or the state government.

Although most of us have a distaste for leaving our wealth to the government, is it wise to leave it all to your children?

A wealthy businessman sought counsel from me (Larry). He had been successful financially and had a sizable estate. When I asked him what he planned to do with it all, he replied, "I'll leave it to my children, I guess."

I then asked him why he didn't just give it to them right then, and he replied, "Why, they don't know how to handle money. They'd just lose it all!"

Becoming a bit bolder, I ventured, "Do you think they would lose it after you died as well?"

The businessman responded, "Well, I'll be gone then, so who cares?" We believe that you should care as part of your life overview. God cares, because being a good steward doesn't have to stop with death.

Most of us have the ability to create an estate today. You may not have as sizable an estate as this gentleman, but you may have land, a 401(k), IRAs, a house, and a life insurance policy. Your estate may be worth more than you think.

The common strategy with most people, including Christians, is to keep as much as possible while they're alive, then leave it all to their heirs upon their death. Unfortunately the heirs are usually poorly trained to manage the assets. Wouldn't it be a shame for your wealth to ruin your children or grandchildren? *"An inheritance gained hurriedly at the beginning will not be blessed in the end"* (Proverbs 20:21).

Warren Buffet, the famous billionaire investor, is the world's second-richest man. He calls inherited wealth "food stamps for the rich." Noted for his financial common sense, he said, "All these people who think that food stamps are debilitating and lead to a cycle of poverty, they're the same ones who go out and want to leave a ton of money to their kids." Buffet later rebutted the rumor that his kids were written out of his will. He said that they've gotten gifts right along, but are not going to live the lives of the super rich.[3]

Decision 2: Treatment—Do you treat heirs the same? As you contemplate your estate and heirs, you may realize that some of your children are much better equipped to handle wealth than others. You may reflect upon your family situation and realize that some have more genuine needs than others. These thoughts may conflict with your notion that you have to treat each heir the same.

We would suggest that you love your children equally and, as such, you treat them uniquely. All children, spouses, and grandchildren are unique. They are unique in their character, values, ability to deal with life, vocation, health, and own family situation. To treat unique people exactly the same may actually be dishonoring to them.

We recommend asking yourself the following questions as you consider transferring wealth.

1. What is the worst thing that can happen if I transfer wealth to _____?

2. How serious is it?

3. How likely is it to occur?

You can then repeat the questions in a more positive frame of mind, starting with, "What is the best thing that can happen if I transfer wealth to _____?"

Decision 3: Timing—Now or later or both? Let's say that you have been active in supporting a ministry through your volunteer efforts for many years. Let's further assume you have enough wealth to last your lifetime, and you plan to give a substantial gift to the ministry upon your death as mentioned in your will.

The ministry has a current need to complete an obvious God-directed mission. You may outlive the usefulness of that ministry, and your gift may not be needed as much later as it is now.

A similar situation could be true with your heirs. They may have more need for your inheritance now than when they are fifty. The key principle here is to time the transfer of your assets to maximize their use by you, your heirs, and Kingdom servants. Essentially, "do your givin' while you're livin' so you're knowin' where it's goin'."

If you want to include your children in your will but are unsure about their ability to handle money, consider giving them token inheritances while you are alive.

One of the best things about giving money to your children (or grandchildren) is that you get to watch them use it to enrich their lives. Unfortunately, lifetime giving also means you have to watch them make mistakes.

For some parents and grandparents, this poses a challenge. Instead of giving money freely, we may be tempted to want something in return: phone calls, visits during the holidays, a license to meddle in our children's marriages, and so on. But those kinds of expectations run contrary to the spirit of generous living. When you make a gift to your children, be sure it is exactly that: a gift.

Decision 4: Title—What? Make an inventory list of your assets. Begin considering the specific items you want to pass to children or to charity. It is your wealth—for a time. Ultimately, God owns it all. When considering wealth transfer, you are not transferring ownership, but you are transferring a stewardship interest. Understanding this changes the paradigm of when, how, and how much to transfer.

Decision 5: Tools and Techniques—Trusts, wills, CRATs, CRUTs, ILITs, foundations. Too often much of the wealth transfer or estate planning process erroneously begins with tools and techniques to control taxes. Decision 5 should come after decisions 1–4. The tools and techniques become the focus of planning rather than a tool of planning. They are the means, not the ends. Although sophisticated tools and trusts are useful, you should not let your lawyer, insurance agent, accountant, or financial planner distract you. Make the first four decisions; then use the tools and techniques.

Rather than rely on a trust, build trust with your heirs and charities. Are you using a trust for good purposes, or do you not trust the use of the transferred assets by the recipients? Avoid trying to control wealth beyond the grave. Still, using these various tools wisely, you can achieve, and perhaps leverage, a wise wealth transfer. Some ministries and charities provide free assistance in using these tools if you include them as beneficiaries.

Decision 6: Talk—Open communication. This can be a challenge for most families. It is hard enough to talk about money, but to talk about money and death is even harder. First, you and your spouse should talk about how much to leave children, grandchildren, each other, and charity. God desires that a husband and wife have unity in their decision making. Remember that God did not give you a spouse to frustrate you but to complete you.

Beyond communication with your spouse, communicate with other family members. Every family has a family conference in the attorney's office after a death occurs to read a will. Wouldn't it be far better to have the family conference prior to death? Then you can have an opportunity to teach and train and explain your reasoning to your heirs.

A family conference can be an invaluable time of bringing a family closer together. Parents, children, and grandchildren can understand one another better. For the heirs it is important to establish proper expectations. An heir may have difficulty coping with a gift that is significantly different from his or her expectations. Let's say that a child is expecting $200,000 but only receives $20,000. The surprise may be difficult for the child to deal with. Hopefully, the child hadn't spent that money yet!

LEAVING OR OVERSEEING A LEGACY?

God leaves no subject untouched in His Word and, fortunately, that includes inheritance. Even a brief survey of the Bible reveals that God provided for each generation through inheritance.

In biblical times the sons inherited their fathers' properties and thus provided for the rest of their families. What is not so obvious is that in most instances, the sons received their inheritances while their fathers were still living, enabling the fathers to oversee their sons' stewardship.

It would be interesting to see how money-management training would be different if parents knew that one day the estate would be in the children's hands and the parents would have to depend on them for their support.

Good stewardship includes providing an inheritance for your family and being sure that every family member knows how to manage it. It is so easy to procrastinate. It's a "tyranny of the urgent" problem that keeps us from doing the important items. If you have not prepared a will, *now* is the time to do it.

These decisions are not easy. Ask God to lead you in your decisions. I (Ron) remember being asked a difficult question after a speaking engagement.

A wealthy couple approached me. They had had three children, including a son who was involved in an immoral, irresponsible lifestyle. The couple had heard me speak about these issues of wealth transfer. In the interest of what they thought was "good stewardship," they had all but decided to leave the wayward child out of their wills. Giving him money, they reasoned, would be tantamount to wasting God's resources.

The only problem was that they did not feel comfortable about the decision. They had prayed about it and sought the advice of several wise and mature Christians, yet they still struggled emotionally with the idea of disinheriting their son. They asked me what I thought they should do.

I immediately breathed a quick prayer: "Lord, help!" Then, prompted by the Holy Spirit, I asked the couple a pointed question. "Would your son be more likely to repent and come to Christ if he were disinherited, and understood why, or if you were to include him in your wills?"

The couple replied without hesitation. "He'd be more likely to come to Christ if he was in our wills. But our assets belong to God. We can't just use them to benefit our son, can we?"

Instead of answering that question, I asked another one: "Do you think God would spend the amount that you would leave your son in order to encourage him to become a Christian?"

I could see the light dawn in their eyes. "Yes," they said, "He would." And with that, it became an easy decision. They would include their son in their wills.

In this case, asking the right questions made all the difference in the couple's financial decision. Sometimes, though, you can be too close to an issue, emotionally speaking, to think clearly and ask the right questions. When that happens, it is important to pray diligently for God's direction and to seek professional counsel from a Christian perspective.

Whether it is deciding how to plan your estate or manage your investments, we agree with the following counsel by the great teacher William Arthur Ward:

> Before you speak, listen. Before you write, think. Before you spend, earn. Before you invest, investigate. Before you criticize, wait. Before you pray, forgive. Before you quit, try. Before you retire, save. Before you die, give.

ASK LARRY

Q. We would like to leave a sizable bequest to several charitable organizations. We also wish to be wise in our giving. In selecting the charities, what are some questions we should ask? How do we know our money will be used wisely?

A. Each Christian must ask some fundamental questions before giving God's money to any organization, whether Christian or secular. This requires the application of God's wisdom and good common sense. *"The plans of the heart belong to the man, but the answer of the tongue is from the LORD"* (Proverbs 16:1). Just because you are asked to give doesn't mean that giving to that organization is God's plan for you. Ask for God's direction about your giving. *"But if any of you lacks wisdom, let him ask of God, who gives to all generously . . . and it will be given to him"* (James 1:5).

Here are a few guidelines for giving to an organization.

1. Who is asking for the funds? If you are not personally familiar with exactly what the organization does, get a list of references from the organization that can be verified through other well-known groups. Ask for a doctrinal statement to determine whether the ministry is communicating a message true to God's Word. Are the lives of the leaders consistent with scriptural principles? Notice how people respond to the message. Are goals being accomplished, and is the ministry bearing fruit?

2. For what purpose will the funds be used? Is the organization multiplying itself? Ask for a projected budget. At times you may want to specify exactly where your gift will be applied.

3. How are funds raised and managed? Ask if a fund-raising group is involved and what percentage of the funds go to that group. If more than 25 percent of the resources are being used for fund-raising, be suspicious. Two indicators of good financial management practices are a low debt/income ratio and minimal changes in overhead expenses from year to year. Definitely avoid giving to ministries that use high-pressure fund raising techniques or questionable gimmicks (special delivery letters, telegrams, or "miracle" items).

4. Request a copy of the ministry's annual budget and an audited financial statement for the previous year. Check to see if it is a member of the Evangelical Council for Financial Accountability (ECFA).

5. Above all, do you believe God is leading you to give to that organization (see 2 Corinthians 9:7)?

ASK RON

Q. Do you have any provisions in your will for charitable bequests?

A. Absolutely! What Judy and I have done is figure out how much we are going to leave to each child. This is an absolute amount, not a percentage of our estate. Then everything above that is going to charity.

We figured an absolute dollar amount because our estate value could vary because of the value of our businesses and other factors. We would not want to risk ruining our kids if we left all of the inheritance to them; we love them too much to take that risk. Our goal is to transfer wisdom as well as wealth.

And we feel God has called us to be concerned about building His Kingdom. Once you have adequately—or in many cases today, more than adequately—provided for children and grandchildren, you can feel the freedom and joy in funding God's work. The ministries and charities that Judy and I support do work that we can't do after our deaths.

ASK LARRY

Q. What are some practical ways you worked with your children and helped them with investing?

A. I think the risk-reward system of our economy can be clearly demonstrated to your children by entrusting to them a sum of money, small at first, to be invested. What better way for a teenager or young adult to see how real the economy and markets are than to put some of their money at risk.

I helped each of our sons get involved in an area of investing to demonstrate how free enterprise really works. For one son, it was a car to fix up and resell. For another, it was repairing and reselling a small rental house. With a third one, it was a small coin collection. The financial cost to me was relatively small, but the reward was helping to develop three free-market enthusiasts.

ASK YOURSELF

- How much money do I plan to leave to my children?
- Do they have the wisdom to handle an inheritance?
- Though not wrong, is leaving an inheritance for my children wise?
- How much money do I want to leave to charities and/or ministries?
- How and when do I want to distribute this inheritance?
- Do my children or grandchildren have any special needs that God might want me to provide for?
- Who will serve as executor of my will?
- Who will manage my affairs for me if I become incapacitated and unable to do so?
- Have I discussed my wealth-transfer plans with my spouse and heirs?

CONCLUSION
— OR —
"Take Hold of the Life That Is Truly Life"

The hardest struggle of all is to be something different
from what the average man is.
CHARLES M. SCHWAB

Money never made a man happy yet, nor will it. There is nothing in its
nature to produce happiness. The more a man has, the more he wants.
Instead of its filling a vacuum, it makes one. If it satisfies one want, it
doubles and trebles that want another way. That was a true proverb of
the wise man, rely upon it; "Better is little with the fear of the Lord,
than great treasure, and trouble therewith."
BENJAMIN FRANKLIN

Why would you settle for such brief, short-term, inadequate, low-yield
dividend pleasures offered by the world when eternal pleasures—tens of
thousands of years of pleasures—await?
HEARD FROM THE PULPIT OF AN ANONYMOUS PASTOR

"Do not store up for yourselves treasures on earth, where moth and
rust destroy, and where thieves break in and steal. But store up for
yourselves treasures in heaven, where neither moth nor rust destroys,
and where thieves do not break in or steal."
MATTHEW 6:19–20

The media refer to "the graying of America." Sociologists analyze "the coming of age of the baby boomers." The politically correct would say we are "chronologically challenged." Really, we are just plain growing old.

We are learning to be content with that. As someone recently reminded us in an e-mail, there are some good things about getting older.

- Your investment in health insurance is finally beginning to pay off.
- Your secrets are safe with your friends because they can't remember them either.
- Your supply of brain cells is finally down to a manageable size.
- Your eyes won't get much worse.
- People no longer view you as a hypochondriac.
- Things you buy now won't wear out.
- There's nothing left to learn the hard way.
- Your joints are more accurate than the National Weather Service.
- In a hostage situation you are likely to be released first.
- You are smarter, *much smarter,* at fifty-plus than when you were only twenty-five.

Rather than approaching the second half of life with dread or fear, see it as a great adventure with the Lord. Think of the wisdom you have learned throughout your life—some earned by a degree from the School of Hard Knocks and some earned by prudently following biblical counsel and teaching.

At every stage, the demographic phenomenon of the baby boomer generation has made a great impact on American society. With increased prosperity and longevity, will your wealth and life have a lasting impact on your family and the Kingdom?

Avoid fitting in with what Ralph Waldo Emerson described when he said, "We are always getting ready to live but never living." Take hold of the life that is truly life—the abundant life available through a personal relationship with the Creator God and His Son, Jesus Christ.

As our friend Bob Buford said, "Do you want to get to the end of your life, stand before God, and hear Him say, 'So what'? No, you want Him to tell you, 'Well done.'"

We have purposed in this book to share all the financial wisdom we possess, all the wisdom we could borrow from others, and all the wisdom available in God's Word. Our recommendations may vary from the world's advice. We encourage you to keep working in some capacity during retirement, though the world says you are entitled to leisure. We recommend to pay off debt, though others give reasons to keep or increase debt. We recommend diversifying to preserve, though the secular instinct is to get rich quick.

It is hard to go against the grain of a materialistic, status-seeking society. The story of Mr. and Mrs. Thing provides a vivid reminder of truth.

> Mr. and Mrs. Thing are a very pleasant and successful couple.
>
> At least, that's the verdict of most people who tend to measure success with a "thingometer."
>
> When the "thingometer" is put to work in the life of Mr. and Mrs. Thing, the result is startling.
>
> There is Mr. Thing sitting down on a luxurious and very expensive thing, almost hidden by a large number of other things.
>
> Things to sit on, things to sit at, things to cook on, things to eat from, all shiny and new.
>
> Things, things, things.
>
> Things to clean with and things to wash with and things to clean and things to wash.
>
> And things to amuse and things to give pleasure and things to watch and things to play.

Things for the long, hot summer and things for the short, cold winter.

Things for the big thing in which they live and things for the garden and things for the deck and things for the kitchen and things for the bedroom.

And things on four wheels and things on two wheels and things to put on top of the four wheels and things to pull behind the four wheels and things to add to the interior of the thing on four wheels.

Things, things, things.

And there in the middle are Mr. and Mrs. Thing, smiling and pleased as punch with things, thinking of more things to add to things.

Secure in their castle of things.

Do they sound familiar? The story of Mr. and Mrs. Thing always strikes a chord with the audience when shared in a public forum. Everyone, it seems, knows someone who fits their description. (And all of us probably see something of ourselves in this couple.)

Mr. and Mrs. Thing may be secure in their castle of things, but that's not the end of their story. Here it is:

Well, I just want you to know that your things can't last.

They're going to pass. There's going to be an end to them.

Oh, maybe an error in judgment, maybe a temporary loss of concentration,

Or maybe you'll just pass them off to the secondhand thing dealer.

Or maybe they'll wind up a mass of mangled metal being towed off to the thing yard.

And what about the things in your house?

Well, it's time for bed.

Put out the cat, make sure you lock the door so some thing-
    taker doesn't come and take your things.

And that's the way life goes, doesn't it?

And someday, when you die, they only put one thing in the
    box.

You.

—Anonymous

We hope that the legacy of this book will live on in the legacy of your life and wealth. May the Lord bless you indeed and cause your wealth to last.

NOTES

Introduction

1. Allstate Financial's "Retirement Reality Check" survey in conjunction with Harris Interactive. Harris randomly polled fourteen hundred people born between 1946 and 1961 with household incomes ranging from $35,000 to $100,000. Two hundred African-Americans and two hundred Hispanics were interviewed as part of the total sample surveyed.

2. Story paraphrased from 2 Kings 4:1–7.

Chapter 1: Is This Economy Different?

1. "Past Crises Offer Hope for Economy, Warnings to Watch," *The Wall Street Journal,* 26 September 2002.

2. National Bureau of Economic Research, Business Cycle Dating Committee, www.nber.org.

3. Ibid.

4. Results based on the Standard & Poor's 500 Index of the five hundred largest stocks on all U.S. markets for the respective period. Assume income dividends were reinvested.

5. Results based on the NASDAQ Composite Index for the respective period.

6. Results based on the Standard & Poor's 500 Index of the five hundred largest stocks on all U.S. markets for the respective period. Assume income dividends were reinvested.

7. Results based on the NASDAQ Composite Index for the respective period.

8. Economic History Services, John J. McCusker, "What Was the Inflation Rate Then?" 2001, URL: http://www.eh.net/hmit/inflation/

9. James K. Glassman and Kevin A. Hassett, "Stock Prices Are Still Far Too Low," *The Wall Street Journal,* 17 March 1999.

10. Morris Mandel, compiler, *Stories for Public Speakers* [Abridged] (New York: Jonathan David Publishers, 1996).

Chapter 2: Planning to Last

1. Henry T. Blackaby and Claude V. King, *Experiencing God* (Nashville: LifeWay Press, 1990) n.p..

Chapter 3: The Decision-Making Process

1. Robert T. Kiyosaki with Sharon Lechter, C.P.A., *Rich Dad, Poor Dad* (New York: Warner Books, 1997), 80.

2. Our knowledge of James's concept was through a gospel tract written by psychologist Henry Brandt. Brandt used this scenario to explain that until we make a decision to trust Jesus Christ as our Savior, we are in Life's *Greatest* Living Option. We have a choice to make: to receive Him and His gift of eternal life or to continue life without Him. God has given us the ability to choose. There is a consequence to our choice: eternal life in heaven with Him if we receive Him or eternal separation from Him in hell if we reject Him. But, while we are choosing, we are in one of the choices already. We are headed toward eternity without Him.

3. *Executive Leadership Newsletter,* National Institute of Business Management. Dick Biggs, Sucessories Library, "Burn Brightly Without Burning Out."

Chapter 4: Retiring Conventional Wisdom about Retirement

1. Information obtained from the Chick-fil-A company web site at www.chick-fil-a.com.

2. Tom Neven, "A Doer of the Word," *Focus on the Family Magazine,* 2000.

3. Information obtained from the Chick-fil-A company web site at www.chick-fil-a.com.

4. Truett Cathy, *It's Easier to Succeed Than to Fail* (Nashville: Oliver Nelson Publishers, 1989).

5. Jim Dailey, "A Conversation with Truett Cathy," *Decision Magazine,* October 2002.

6. "Brief History of Social Security," Social Security Administration, www.ssa.gov.

7. "History Page Questions and Answers," Social Security on-line, www.ssa.gov.

8. This "at birth" life expectancy measure can be misleading because of the high infant mortality at that time. After a person reached adulthood, many lived beyond sixty-five. The Social Security Administration documented that 6.7 million people were age sixty-five or older in 1930.

9. Peter Drucker, as quoted in the introduction to *Half-Time* by Bob Buford (Zondervan Publishing House, 1994).

10. *National Vital Statistics Reports,* vol. 49, no. 12 for the year 2000 as cited on the Center for Disease Control web site at www.cdc.gov.

11. Billy Graham Evangelistic Association web site, © 2002, www.billygraham.org.

12. "A World of Options: Interview with Peter Drucker," *Halftime Magazine,* September/October 2002, 25.

13. "Aging Well" study by George Vaillant as quoted in *The Wall Street Journal*, 17 September 2002.

Chapter 5: Income to Last

1. "A Profile of Older Americans: 2001," Administration on Aging of the Department of Health and Human Services. Profile is based on data from the U.S. Bureau of the Census.

2. Social Security Administration's (SSA) web site at www.ssa.gov. The amounts shown are the statutory amounts for 2003. These amounts are indexed to inflation and change annually.

3. Ibid.

4. Ellen Schultz, "Workers May Get Help on Pension Choices," *The Wall Street Journal*, 17 October 2002.

5. Ibid.

6. The amount per month was obtained by averaging three leading insurance companies' annuity quotations. The amount varies for each insurer.

Chapter 6: Invest to Last

1. Peter Lynch with John Rothchild, *Beating the Street* (New York: A Fireside Book, A Division of Simon & Schuster, 1994).

Chapter 8: Insurance for Wealth to Last

1. "Beyond 50: A Report to the Nation on Trends in Health Security" (Washington, D.C.: AARP, May 2002).

2. Watson Wyatt Worldwide study as quoted in the Associated Press, 16 September 2002.

3. *Washington Post*, April 1996, and *Your Money*, December/January 2000.

4. Long-Term Care Insurance: A Special Guide from Kiplinger's Retirement Report, June 1999.

5. Health Insurance Association of America (HIAA), Guide to Long-Term Care Insurance, 1996. Also, CNN Financial Network, 26 August 1999.

6. Projected Needs of the Aging Baby Boomers, U.S. General Accounting Office, June 1991, 2.

7. Premiums based on the average of three major national carriers and includes applicable spousal discount.

Chapter 9: What Women Need to Know Before They Are Widows

1. Based on data from the U.S. Bureau of the Census cited in a 2001 report by the Administration on Aging of the Department of Health and Human Services.

Chapter 10: A Legacy to Last

1. CNN, 18 September 1997 (www.cnn.com).

2. Eric Gibson, "Can $100 Million Help Make Poetry Matter?" *TheWall Street Journal,* 26 November 2002.

3. Robynn Tysver, "Warren Buffet Hits Campaign Trail," *San Diego Union-Tribune,* Associated Press, 16 October 1994, I–1.

ABOUT THE AUTHORS

Larry Burkett was born in Winter Park, Florida, on March 3, 1939, the fifth of eight children. After completing high school in Winter Garden, Florida, he entered the U.S. Air Force, where he served as an electronics technician in the Strategic Air Command.

Upon completion of his military duties, he and his wife, Judy, returned to central Florida, where he worked in the space program at Cape Canaveral, Florida. He spent the next several years at the space center in charge of an experiments test facility that served the Mercury-, Gemini-, and Apollo-manned space programs. While working in the space center, Larry earned degrees in marketing and finance at Rollins College, Winter Park, Florida.

Larry left the space center in 1970 to become vice president of an electronics manufacturing firm. In 1972 Larry put his trust and faith in Jesus Christ to guide his life—an event that had a profound effect. In 1973 he left the electronics company to join the staff of a nonprofit ministry, Campus Crusade for Christ, as a financial counselor. It was during this time that he began an intense study of what the Bible says about handling money, and he started teaching small groups around the country.

In 1976 Larry left the campus ministry to form Christian Financial Concepts, a nonprofit organization dedicated to teaching the biblical principles of handling money. CFC has now grown to a nationwide ministry that reaches literally millions of people.

Larry authored more than seventy books, sales of which now exceed 11 million copies and include several national best-sellers. The daily radio broadcasts, "Money Matters" and "How to Manage Your Money," are carried on more than 1,100 radio outlets worldwide. In May 1996, Southwest Baptist University conferred an Honorary Doctorate in Economics on Larry.

The late Larry Burkett leaves wife, Judy, four grown children and nine grandchildren.

Ron Blue is president of Christian Financial Planning Institute. Following his graduation from Indiana University with a Masters of Business Administration degree, Ron joined the management group of Peat, Marwick, Mitchell & Co. and worked with the firm in New York, Dallas, and San Francisco.

In 1970, Ron founded an Indianapolis-based CPA firm that has grown to be one of the fifty largest CPA firms in the United States. Leaving the firm in 1977, Ron became administrative vice president of Leadership Dynamics International. While with Leadership Dynamics, he was involved in developing and teaching biblically based leadership and management seminars in the United States and Africa.

Convinced that Christians would better handle their personal finances if they were counseled objectively with the highest technical expertise and from a biblical perspective, he founded a financial planning firm in 1979. That firm grew to manage over over $2.5 billion in assets for its more than 5,000 clients nationwide with a staff of more than 175 people in fourteen regional offices.

Ron retired from Ronald Blue & Co. in 2003 in order to lead an international effort to equip and motivate Christian financial professionals to serve the body of Christ by implementing biblical wisdom in their lives and practices. This venture has resulted in financial freedom and increased giving by multiplied thousands of Christians.

Ron is the author of nine books on personal finance from a biblical perspective, including the best-seller *Master Your Money*, first published in 1986 and now in its twenty-ninth printing. He is featured in the popular, six-part Master Your Money video series, produced by Walk Thru the Bible Ministries and used in more than 5,500 churches across the country.

Ron has appeared on numerous radio and television programs, including "Focus on the Family," "Family News in Focus," "The 700 Club," "Prime Time America," and "Moody Radio Open Line." He is a regular contributor to several national Christian magazines.

Ron currently serves on the boards of directors of Campus Crusade for Christ, Crown Financial Ministries, the National Christian Foundation, and Thomas Nelson, Inc., a New York Stock Exchange listed company. He also serves on the boards of trustees of the Maclellan Foundation and the Sandra and William B. Johnson Foundation, Inc. He formerly served on the boards of directors of Family Research Council, Promise Keepers, Insight for Living, the Medical Institute, and Walk Thru the Bible Ministries.

In 2002, Ron received the Honors Award from the Georgia chapter of the Financial Planning Association (FPA). In 2003, he received the honored designation of Distinguished Entrepreneur from the Indiana University Kelley School of Business, his alma mater.

Ron and Judy live in Atlanta. They have five children and six grandchildren.

Jeremy L. White has been a Certified Public Accountant for fifteen years with financial experience in public accounting and industry. His CPA firm specializes in retirement planning and wealth management for those in the second half of life.

Jeremy has been a contributor for the past five years to Larry Burkett's *Money Matters* newsletter. He assisted Larry and Crown Financial Ministries as the primary writing consultant in updating their successful workbook, *Family Financial Planning*. He has been a frequent guest on the "How to Manage Your Money" radio broadcast.

Before founding his own financial firm, Jeremy worked with the national accounting firm of Ernst & Young in their Miami, Florida office.

Jeremy's firm also provides tax preparation, small business advisory services, estate planning, and financial counseling. His office can be reached at 1-888-296-5616. For free tax tips and an archive of articles, see his web site at www.consultcpa.com.

Jeremy and his wife, Sharon, live in Paducah, Kentucky, with their two daughters, Jenaye and Jaclyn.